SRA
Reading Mastery
Signature Edition

D1547155

Language Arts
Teacher's Guide
Grade 1

Siegfried Engelmann
Jean Osborn
Karen Lou Seitz Davis

McGraw Hill SRA

Columbus, OH

The **McGraw·Hill** Companies

Contents

STORY GRAMMAR AND LITERATURE STRAND

WRITING STRAND

APPENDICES

Introduction

PROGRAM ORGANIZATION

Reading Mastery Signature Edition, Grade 1 Language Arts presents three main strands. During each lesson, the program presents exercises from more than one strand. Each lesson throughout the program has several exercises from the **Language Concepts Strand.** This strand teaches language concepts such as classification skills, analogies, questioning skills, and skills in describing things. The program also has a strand that teaches **Story Grammar and Literature**. This strand provides frequent opportunities for children to predict what characters will do (based on information about what they have done in earlier stories). Finally, the program has a **Writing Strand**, which presents story-related sentence writing, cooperative story writing, main idea sentence writing and sequence sentence writing.

The Grade 1 Language Arts Scope and Sequence chart that follows summarizes the content of each of three strands.

LANGUAGE 1 SCOPE AND SEQUENCE CHART, Lessons 1–130

Lessons 1 5 10 15

Language Concepts	**Actions**	(10–75, 104–105)	
	Classification	(1–50, 60, 73, 82–130)	
	Word Skills	Opposites (1–40, 58–72, 98–100, 130)	
		Definitions (41–130)	
		Synonyms (77–130)	
		Contractions (120–130)	
	Sentence Skills	How-Who-What-Where-When-Why (1–130)	
		Questioning Skills (20–130)	
		Verb Tense (97–130)	
		Statements (60–75) (95–130)	
	Reasoning Skills	Same-Different (7–17) (75–80)	
		True-False (15–20) (26–27) (40–80)	
		Can Do (40–85)	
		Only (18–45)	
		Description (113–115)	
		Analogies (50–130)	
		Questioning Skills (20–127)	
		If-Then (45–50) (59–60)	
	Directional Skills	From-To (35–50)	
		Map Reading (47–120)	
	Information	Days, Months, Seasons (1–130)	
		Materials (15–36) (50–57)	
	Applications	Absurdities (6–130)	
		Temporal Sequencing (14–36) (49–50)	
	Additional Tracks in the Workbook	Coloring (1–130)	
		Part-Whole (3–5)	
		Locations (7–40) (50–65)	
		Writing Opposites	
Story Grammar and Literature Strand	**Story Grammar**	Stories (1–65)	
		Extending Story Grammar (44–45)	
		Character Identification (15–18) (56–58) (70–73) (95–97) (118–120) (122–123)	
	Story Completion and Plays	Storytelling Details (1–80)	
		Sequencing Events (6–55)	
		Data Collection (41–42) (49–51) (86–87)	
		Extrapolation (11–13)(16–20)(25–27)(29–30) (31–32) (34–36) (66–67) (70–71) (84–86)	
		Putting on a Play (40–80)	
		Skills (Days, Months, Bleep Talk) (57–64)	
		Story Completion (62–66) (76–78) (114–116) (126–127)	
Writing Strand	**Story-Related Writing**	Sentence Construction and Writing (51–55, 61–64, 73–78, 87, 102)	
		Cooperative Story Writing (130)	
	Main Idea Sentence Writing	(80–130)	
	Sequence Sentence Writing	(120)	

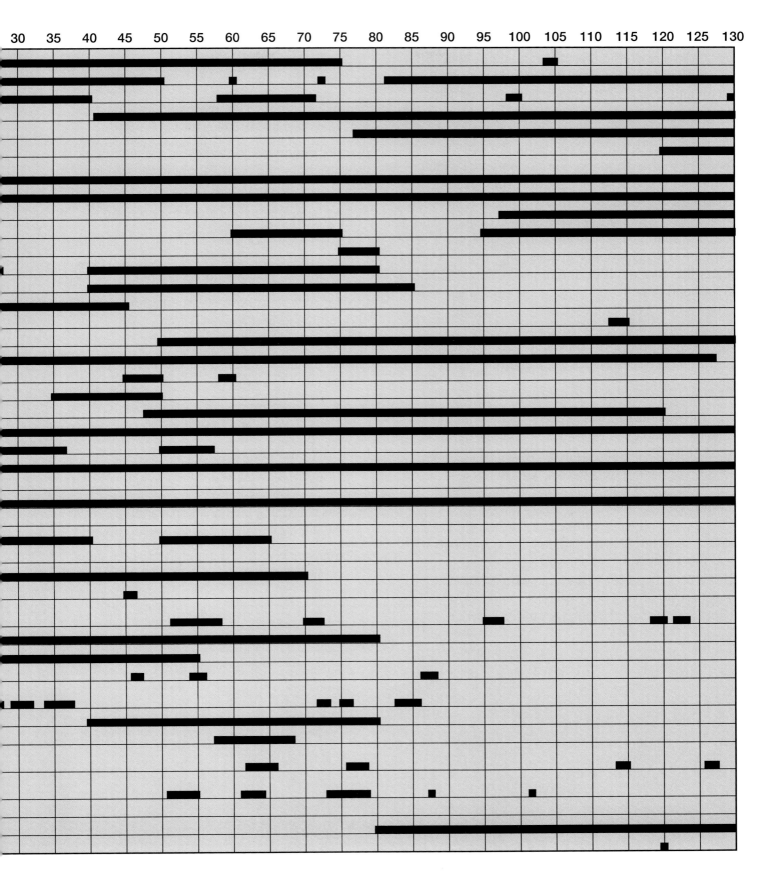

Schedule

The Grade 1 Language Arts component is not to be scheduled during the daily reading period. Periods for the language arts program require 30–45 minutes per day (the same time requirements as periods for the reading program).

The language component should never take priority over the reading program. If you try to teach both the language component and reading component in the same period, you will not complete the reading program during the first-grade year. Students will therefore be behind in reading during the following year. Grade 1 Language Arts contains 130 lessons, which is fewer than the number of reading lessons (160). This means that if you start the language arts program on the same day that you start the reading program, and if you teach one lesson a day in each program, you will finish the language program before the reading program.

For Whom

Grade 1 Language Arts is appropriate for all children who have completed the kindergarten level of the *Signature Edition.* Note that children may be placed in the Grade 1 Language Arts program even if they did not go through the K language program.

To determine whether these children have the skills needed to place in Grade 1 Language Arts, test these children using the placement test (see page 97 of this guide). Students who make five or fewer errors on this test have skills needed to begin the Grade 1 Language Arts program.

Special Features

Grade 1 Language Arts is a comprehensive language program. Its special features include:

- a Direct Instruction approach to the teaching of a wide range of important language concepts and skills;

- carefully organized sequences of exercises that make up the daily lessons;

- teacher directions for the clear presentation of the concepts and skills taught in the program;

- frequent opportunities for both group and individual practice on what is being taught;

- statement repetition exercises that help children become practiced with both the concepts and statements of the language of school;

- the application of newly learned language concepts and thinking skills to problem-solving activities;

- stories that introduce model stories with unique story grammar;

- a wide assortment of writing activities, including story-related writing;

- a continuous integration and review of all the concepts and skills that appear in the program;

- workbook activities that teach new concepts and skills and that give children opportunities to apply what they are learning to new contexts;

- a placement test that evaluates the entry level of the students.

Teacher's Presentation Books

The teacher's presentation books contain the daily lessons you will present to the children. These books also contain directions for the workbook activities, as well as the stories that were written especially for the program.

The daily lessons are divided into two teacher's presentation books.

Book A   Lessons 1–60

Book B   Lessons 61–130

Teacher's Guide

You are reading the teacher's guide. The guide provides directions for how to use the program materials and how to implement the program in your classroom. In addition, the teacher's guide summarizes the content of the program and describes useful teaching techniques and specific correction procedures for a number of the exercises in the daily lessons.

The teacher's guide also includes the placement test (the results determine which children should be placed in the program).

Student's Workbook

The workbook also contains activities the children do as part of each lesson. Some of the workbook activities are done under your directions, and some are done as independent seat work. Each child in the class will need a workbook.

Additional Materials

Answer Key This key provides the answers to the workbook lessons.

Teaching the Program

GETTING STARTED

Use of Materials

A lesson should be scheduled for each instructional group on every available school day. Allow 30-45 minutes each day for each group's lesson, which includes five to ten minutes for independent workbook activities.

The Teacher's Presentation Books

The teacher's presentation books provide you with directions for teaching each of the 130 lessons in the program. Here is some information about these books:

- The presentation books are divided into lessons. The number of the lesson appears in the upper left corner of the first page of the lesson.

- The lessons are divided into exercises.

- The exercise heading indicates the track name, that is, the concept the exercise focuses on.

- What you are to say is in blue type.

- What you and the children are to do is in black type enclosed in parentheses.

- The oral response expected from the children is in italics.

LESSON **29**

Objectives

- Generate statements to describe actions using present and past tense. (Exercise 1)
- Answer questions about previously learned calendar facts. (Exercise 2)
- Given two classes, identify which class is biggest, describe why and name members of the biggest class. (Exercise 3)
- Name common opposites, answer questions by generating sentences using opposites and **generate a sentence that means the opposite of a given sentence.** (Exercise 4)
- **Given a sequence, answer questions about the sequence.** (Exercise 5)
- Given two objects, identify whether a statement is true of "only one" or "both" objects. (Exercise 6)
- Given a calendar, identify the day and date for "yesterday" and "today." (Exercise 7)
- Relate a familiar story grammar to a picture that indicates the sequence of events for a new story. (Exercise 8)
- Ask questions involving "class," "use" and "materials" to figure out a "mystery" object. (Exercise 9)
- **Follow coloring rules involving some and all.** (Exercise 10)

EXERCISE 1 Actions

1. Here's an action game.
2. Watch me. (Touch the floor and continue touching it.)
- What am I touching? (Signal.) *The floor.*
3. (Stop touching the floor. Touch your chair and continue touching it.)
- What am I doing now? (Signal.) *Touching your chair.*
- What did I do **before** I touched my chair? (Signal.) *Touched the floor.*
- Yes, I touched the floor.
4. Say the whole thing about what I did before I touched my chair. Get ready. (Signal.) *You touched the floor.*
- What am I doing now? (Signal.) *Touching your chair.*
- Say the whole thing about what I am doing. Get ready. (Signal.) *You are touching your chair.*

EXERCISE 2 Calendar Facts

1. How many months are in a year? (Signal.) *12.*
- Say the fact. Get ready. (Signal.) *There are 12 months in a year.*
- How many seasons are in a year? (Signal.) *Four.*
- Say the fact. Get ready. (Signal.) *There are four seasons in a year.*
- How many days are in a year? (Signal.) *365.*
- Say the fact. Get ready. (Signal.) *There are 365 days in a year.*
- How many weeks are in a year? (Signal.) *52.*
- Everybody, say that fact. Get ready. (Signal.) *There are 52 weeks in a year.*
2. Say the seasons of the year. Get ready. (Signal.) *Winter, spring, summer, fall.*
- Say the months of the year. Get ready. (Signal.) *January, February, March, April, May, June, July, August, September, October, November, December.*

Lesson 29   **151**

Workbook Directions

Workbook activity directions appear at the end of each lesson in the teacher's presentation book, starting with lesson 1. These activities are to be completed in class as part of the daily language lesson, and the finished worksheet is to be taken home.

The Placement Test

Before you begin instruction in Grade 1 Language Arts, the placement test is to be administered individually to each child who has not completed the kindergarten language program. Testing should be completed during the first week of school. The placement test, a sample scoring sheet, and directions for giving and scoring the test appear in Appendix A, pages 98-100, of this guide.

Instructional Grouping

If possible, students should be in smaller groups; ideally, the same groups they are in for reading. If such grouping is not possible, teach the language arts component to the entire class and try to find time to give the low performers extra practice.

Recognize that teaching to the entire class is more difficult because it is harder for you to observe each child. It is important to make sure all of your children are understanding the language concepts and mastering statement-production tasks.

Children Who Have Not Gone Through the Kindergarten Language Arts Program

If children did not go through the kindergarten language arts program, plan to spend most of the time in your first sessions teaching the children to follow your signals and to use the response conventions that occur in the language programs. You can do this by teaching exercises 1 through 7 of lesson 1 in Grade 1 Language Arts. Concentrate on teaching the children to respond to your hand and auditory signals, and to respond in partial or full statements as indicated in various parts of each exercise. On the next day, reteach any of the exercises of lesson 1 that presented problems and finish the rest of the lesson.

Children who have not gone through the kindergarten language program and pass the placement test may have the general language skills necessary for successful performance in the first grade level, but may not know some of the specific information that was taught in the kindergarten program.

For example, some children may not know the names of the days, months, and seasons. It will take more than one lesson to learn these facts.

Children may have trouble in the Classification exercises with words such as *vehicles* and *containers*. If they do, you will need to teach them this vocabulary. Say, **Listen. I'll tell you what class a car, a truck, a bus, a plane, and a bicycle are in—vehicles. All those objects are vehicles. A car is a vehicle. A truck is a vehicle. A bus, a plane, and a bicycle are vehicles. Can anyone else think of another vehicle?** Praise all good responses. Repeat this procedure for several days. Use it with any of the classification terms the children do not know.

Follow similar procedures to teach any vocabulary or concepts that the children will need to know to proceed successfully through the program.

Teaching Children Whose First Language Is Not English

Non-English speakers should start in the kindergarten level of the program. If this is not possible, present the activities from the Kindergarten action track during the first week of instruction. Then teach the first ten complete lessons from the Kindergarten level.

Following this work, start lesson 1 of the Grade 1 sequence.

The general guideline is to make sure that the children are very firm on saying the exact responses specified for the exercises. Repeat parts of lessons in which the children have trouble.

CLASSROOM ORGANIZATION

To organize the children for Grade 1 Language Arts instruction, follow these directions:

1. If you group the children for instruction, seat the children in a curved row. Sit so that you can observe every child in the group as well as the other members of the class. For larger groups, seat the children in two rows.

2. Arrange children according to their instructional needs. Seat the children who need the most help directly in front of you (in the first row if there is more than one row). Seat the children who are likely to need the least help at the ends of the first row (or in the second row). You will naturally look most frequently at the children seated directly in front of you. If you are constantly aware of these children, you will be in a position to know when their responses are firm. When their responses are firm, you can be sure that the rest of the group is firm.

3. Assign seats. Children should sit in their assigned seats every day.

4. Sit close to the children. Position the children as close together as possible.

5. If you are teaching the entire class, seat the lowest performers in front. Monitor their performance carefully.

TEACHING EFFECTIVELY

Getting Into the Lesson

The children respond with enthusiasm when the lesson is well prepared and presented with good pacing. Here are some suggestions that will help you present the lesson:

1. Practice the exercises. Rehearse the exercises before you present them to the children.

2. Get into the lesson quickly. Present the first exercise in the lesson, even if the group is shy or has some behavioral problems. Repeat the exercise until all the children are responding without hesitation. Then quickly present the next exercise.

3. Follow the scripted directions. Present each exercise as it appears in the presentation book. If you change the vocabulary of a particular exercise, the children may have difficulty on future exercises that build on the vocabulary specified in the exercise.

4. Use clear signals. A signal is a motion you make to get a simultaneous response from the group. All signals have the same purpose—to give the children a moment to think and to then enable them to respond together. All signals have the same rationale—if you can get the group to respond simultaneously (with no one child leading the others), you will get information about the performance of all the children, not just those who happen to answer first. Also, all of the children will maximize their opportunities to respond and practice.

5. Practice the signals. Work on signals until they are natural, and you can do them without concentrating on them. Your clear, easy-to-follow signals will help the children follow the steps in the exercises and the sequences of instruction. More information about signals appears in the following section, "Teaching Techniques," pages 12–15.

6. React to the children's responses. Work with the children until their responses are firm and assured. The children should know that they

are doing something important, that you are pleased when they do a good job, and that you will help them when they need help.

7. Pace exercises appropriately. Pacing is the rate at which different parts of the exercises are presented. You and the children should have a sense of moving quickly through the steps of the exercise. The parts of an exercise that are easy for children should be done very briskly. On the other hand, steps in an exercise that are difficult for the children—steps that require them to figure something out—should be presented more slowly. Sometimes the word pause appears in the directions to the teacher. This indicates to you that you should pause an extra second or two to let the children think before you signal the response.

Here are some general guidelines for well-paced instruction:
- Speak quickly and with expression.
- Stress words that are important by saying them louder, not slower.
- Follow the instructions about pausing that appear in the exercise.
- If you miss a line, stumble over words, or rush a signal, repeat that part of the exercise. Tell the children, **"Stop. Let's try that again."**
- Move quickly from one exercise to the next, pausing no longer than three or four seconds between exercises. When the children have done well on the exercise, let them know about it: **"You really did a good job on that part."** Then say, **"New exercise"** and go on to the next exercise.
- If the children are making a lot of errors, slow your pace and pause longer before signaling. This pause gives children more time to think.

What Is Good Performance?

1. The class or group is performing well and deserves praise when:

   - all children respond on signal;

   - all children give the correct answer.

2. When the children respond appropriately,

you should acknowledge it. Specifically,

- praise children when they complete all the steps in an exercise on signal and without making a mistake;

- praise children after they have been corrected. Let them know that now they are right. If the exercise has been particularly difficult and they have worked hard to do it successfully, act particularly pleased: "That was hard. But now you can do it. Good for you";

- praise children only when they perform according to your standards. If you reward a child for poor performance, that child won't be motivated to improve. Furthermore, you will lose your credibility with the other children in the group.

3. Tell the children why you are praising them. After the children have done an entire exercise correctly, say, **"That was good. You did the whole exercise, and it was hard."**

4. Challenge the children. A challenge often motivates a disinterested child to become an eager participant.

If two children perform particularly well, praise them and challenge the other children. **"Wow! Henry and Myrna really can do it. Aren't they good! Just listen to how well they do."**

Firm Responses

Throughout the program you will encounter the following instruction to the teacher: "Repeat until all children's responses are firm." or "Repeat until firm." This instruction means that at the conclusion of every exercise every child should be able to perform the exercise without any need for correction. Children's responses are firm when they give the correct answers at every step of an exercise.

It is easier to bring the children to this standard of performance at the first introduction of an exercise than it will be in a later lesson after they have made the same mistakes many times. It is much more efficient to teach, correct, and repeat until all responses are firm the first time an exercise is presented.

Let the children know what your standard is. Stay with an exercise until you can honestly say to them, **"Good. Everybody can do this exercise."**

Statement Repetition

It is particularly important to work on statement repetition with some children. Children who are able to repeat statements (aloud or to themselves) are more readily able to follow directions successfully and learn from teaching demonstrations that present definitions or rules. Remember, the ability to accurately repeat statements the first time or after only a few practice trials is a good indicator of success in future academic work, including the ability to read and comprehend.

Apply the following standard to evaluate children's statement repetition skill: The child can repeat the statement with every word pronounced acceptably and with all words included.

Do not accept responses in which endings are omitted from words, words are missing, or word order is reversed. Evidence that children have the general idea of the statement is not good enough. They must demonstrate that they have the skill to precisely repeat any statement in each exercise.

The statements in the program have been carefully selected. As the children progress through the program, the statements they learn to use gradually increase in both length and complexity.

Responses to Answers Different from Those in the Book

Although the responses the children are to make are indicated in each exercise, it is quite possible that individual children will make other responses that are equally correct. You should acknowledge all correct responses; you want to let the child who gives another answer to know that his or her observation is a good one. But in teaching the exercise, you will usually have the children respond as the exercise is written.

Here is an example of how to handle a different response: In a Parts exercise a child might call the point of a pencil a tip. You say, **"Right. Some people call this part a tip. But**

it's also called a point. Let's use point. What part is this?"** Continue with the exercise.

There are two reasons for following this practice:
1. Many responses occur across many lessons. The children review them in daily practice.
2. In some tracks a later exercise builds on a response made in an earlier exercise.

Individual Turns

Individual turns are specified at the end of some exercises, but you may use individual turns at the end of any exercise. Here are several suggestions for giving individual turns:

1. Give individual turns only after children's responses are firm. If you wait until the children are firm on group responses, the chances are much better that each child will be able to give a firm response when answering alone.
2. Do not give every child an individual turn for every exercise—two or three individual turns are sufficient unless the exercise is an unusually difficult one. Present individual turns quickly and naturally. You do not need to use a signal; simply ask a question or give an instruction to one child. If you get a correct response, praise the child and then immediately present another question to another child. Don't call on children in a predictable order, starting at one end of the row and calling on every child in turn. Skip around the group.
3. Give most of the turns to the lowest-performing children. By watching those children during the group or class practice of the exercise, you can tell when they are ready to respond individually. When they can do the exercise without further correction, you can safely assume that the other children will be able to do it as well.
4. When a child makes a mistake on an individual turn, present the correction to the entire group. When one child makes a particular mistake, there is probably another child who will make the same mistake. The most efficient remedy, therefore, is to correct the entire group. Then give another individual turn to the child who made the mistake.

5. If you feel doubtful about the responses of any of the children, give individual turns even when they are not specified. On the other hand, if a group does well on an exercise, you may wish to skip individual turns for that exercise.

Progress Through the Program

Here are some questions and answers about the children's progress through Grade 1 Language Arts:

1. How much should you teach each day? Your objective should be to complete one lesson each period. When new concepts are introduced, however, you may not always complete an entire lesson. When the choice is between making sure all the children's responses are firm or completing the lesson in one day, choose firm responses and complete the lesson the next day.

2. What about skipping exercises within lessons? Occasionally you may observe that the children have already learned particular concepts or information. An example: All the children may have a good sense of the calendar facts presented in the Calendar exercises. In that case you do not need to present the Calendar exercise in every lesson in which it appears. Another example: Children frequently find the Opposites review exercises very easy. You can skip some of these exercises or present them as a challenge, saying, "I know you know this. Let's see how quickly we can do this exercise."

HOW TO MAKE THE PROGRAM SUCCEED

Here are some general procedures for making the program work in your classroom:

1. Follow the program. The lessons are carefully organized and sequenced.

2. Follow the suggestions in this teacher's guide for implementing the program and teaching effectively. Study the section of the guide titled *The Program* to learn about the major exercises in each track. Study the correction procedures. Practice presenting the exercises before working with the children.

3. Be sure that every child is responding. Follow the instructions "Repeat until all children's responses are firm."

4. Make sure that the children respond together on signal and that some children are not leading the others. Evaluate the children's responses to determine from their errors if any corrections or additional practice is necessary.

5. Make allowances for regional differences in some of the vocabulary in the exercises: what is referred to as a pop bottle in the Midwest may be called a soda bottle on the East Coast. Some people call a garbage can a trash can. Do not hesitate to make such local substitutions for the words that are used in the program.

6. Relate what the children are learning in the language lesson to what is being done the rest of the day in school. You will find that you will become very conscious of the kind of language you are teaching. Use this language in everyday situations. For example, when you are teaching true/false, you might say, "I'm going to make a true statement about Angela: 'Angela is wearing a yellow sweater.' Now, I'll make a false statement about Sam. 'Sam is wearing a brown shirt.'" When you are teaching if-then rules, you might say, "I'm going to give paper to children if they are sitting down. If you're sitting down, then you get a piece of paper."

TEACHING TECHNIQUES

Signaling the Children's Responses

Why signals? To maximize language practice, it is important for all the children to respond at once. Signals are used so that the children will respond as a group. You will use two signaling techniques to present the exercise and workbook activities—a hand signal and an auditory signal.

An auditory signal is used with workbook exercises. Since the children are looking at a picture in their workbook, they must hear the signal to respond. But when responding to exercises that have no pictures, they are looking at you and will respond to your visual hand signal: You hold out your hand, pause, and then drop your hand. The children respond. The directions in the teacher's presentations books tell you when to signal responses.

The Visual Hand-Drop-Signal The word *signal* after a question or an instruction tells you to drop your hand to signal the children's response.

Hand-drop Signal

Below are the guidelines for giving the visual hand-drop signal:

- At the beginning of each step of the exercise hold out your hand. Keep your hand perfectly still.

- Ask the question or give the instruction.

- Pause about one second, then quickly drop your hand. (The interval between the question or the instruction and the hand drop is the same as that between the question and the touching when using the touch signal.)

- The instant your hand drops, the children are to respond.

Note: If it is easier or more natural for you to tap the book with a pencil, or to clap your hands to signal the children's response, do so. Just be sure that the timing is the same as that described above.

Practicing the Hand-Drop Signal Use the above exercise to practice the hand-drop signal until your "children" are responding together. Watch for these common signaling problems:

- not holding out your hand from the beginning of each step;

- not pausing for one second after you finish talking;

- dropping your hand while you are still talking;

- dropping your hand too slowly.

Auditory Signals For auditory signals, use the same timing you used for visual signals. Talk first, pause, then signal. The pause should be the same length as for visual signals. The auditory signal may be a finger-snap or a tap with a pencil on a part of your book.

CORRECTIONS

All children make mistakes. The mistakes children make provide you with important information about the difficulties they are having. It is important to correct mistakes immediately. Knowing how to effectively correct children's mistakes helps you help the children in your class. Three kinds of correction procedures are used in the program: general corrections, specific corrections, and statement corrections. Each of these is discussed in this section.

General Corrections

Children's responses that call for general corrections include not attending, not answering, and responding before or after the signal. Here are some ideas for correcting these problems.

Not Attending Not attending occurs when children are not listening. Correct not attending by looking at these children and saying, **"Let's try it again."** Then return to the beginning of the exercise. Returning to the beginning of the exercise will help the children understand your standard: Everyone has to pay attention.

Not Responding Not responding occurs when the children don't answer when you signal a response. Some children may learn not to listen the first time a question is asked and then join in later. They may become dependent on the other children's responses and may get the idea they don't have to initiate their own responses. If children are not answering, correct not attending by saying, **"I have to hear everybody."** Then return to the beginning of the exercise.

Responding Before or After the Signal
Remember that the purpose of a signal is to orchestrate a group response. When children do not respond on time (responding before your signal or too long after your signal), they are not attending to your signal, and you are not getting information from every child.

The children will learn to attend to your signal if you consistently return to the beginning of the exercise after each correction. When the children learn that you will repeat the exercise until they are all responding on signal, they will pay more attention to your signal.

If you find that you are spending a lot of time correcting children who are not attending, not responding, and responding before or after the signal, your pacing of the exercise or the signal is probably too slow. Remember that the objective of a signal is not to keep the children sitting on the edges of their seats never knowing when they will have to respond next. Rather, the pacing of signals should be predictable and occurring at a rate that permits children to think and then respond with assurance.

Specific Corrections

Corrections for specific response errors vary from exercise to exercise because these corrections deal with the specific content of a given exercise and the types of errors the children are likely to make. To correct specific response errors, follow the correction procedures that appear in some of the exercises of the teacher's presentation book, as well as in the *Program* section of this guide.

Statement Corrections

The correction procedure for statement errors is consistent from exercise to exercise, even though the statements themselves will vary. You will find that the model, lead, test, and retest correction procedure that is described below really helps children who have trouble making statements.

Here is an example of the statement correction procedure. (Several children have had trouble saying the full statement *"This vehicle is a truck."*)

1. **The model** (Teacher: **"My turn. Listen. This vehicle is a truck."**) In this step you demonstrate the statement the children are to make.

2. **The lead** (Teacher: **"Let's say it together."** You and the children respond together. *"This vehicle is a truck."*) Leading gives the children the benefit of responding with you until they are confident. Some statements require a number of leads to produce a firm, correct response from the children. Don't be afraid to continue leading until the children can produce the statement with you. But remember, the lead step should be used only when the children cannot produce the statement. If they can produce the statement after the model, skip the lead step.

3. **The test** (Teacher: **"Your turn. Say the whole thing."** Children: *"This vehicle is a truck."* If the children say the statement correctly, you know the correction has been effective. If they still have trouble, you know that you must repeat the model and lead steps until all the children can pass the test step.

4. **The retest** This involves going back to an earlier part of the exercise and presenting the subsequent steps to make sure the children can make the statement when it occurs in the context of the entire exercise.

The retest step applies to specific response errors as well. After the children can respond to the specific question or instruction they had previously missed, you should return to an earlier part of the exercise and present the subsequent steps in sequence. The retest is very important. The children will learn that the various steps they take in learning are not isolated, but rather that they fit together in a sequence.

Practicing Corrections It is very important to practice making corrections. You must be able to present a correction without hesitation when the mistake occurs. By practicing the corrections, you will be well prepared for the mistakes that children will commonly make.

Have other adults play the role of the children and make the specified mistake. Then present the correction. Practice it until you can do it quickly and naturally. Also practice returning to the beginning of the exercise and presenting the entire exercise. Your group is firm when they respond correctly to every step of the exercise.

Changing Loud and Draggy Responses

Once the children have mastered a statement form, their statement responses are to be given in a normal, conversational tone.

The children should not shout, nor should they speak in a draggy and unnaturally slow manner. If you find that your group is shouting or is speaking too slowly, you must change these responses to a more acceptable speaking pattern. Follow these steps:

1. Interrupt the loud or draggy responses by saying, **"Stop."**

2. Model a more acceptable way of saying the statement, and tell the children what you are doing. For example: **"Listen. I can say that statement a nice way. This man is holding an umbrella and wearing a hat."** (Slightly exaggerate the modulations and pacing in your model statement.)

3. Lead the children through the statement. Say, **"Let's all say that statement the nice way."** Signal. **"This man is holding an umbrella and wearing a hat."** Repeat the lead until all of the children are saying the statement in an acceptable manner. If any children in the group revert to the loud or draggy response, stop the group and repeat the procedure.

4. Test the children on saying the statement in the acceptable manner. Say, **"All right. Let's hear you say that statement by yourselves. Remember, you're going to say it the nice way."**

Repeat this procedure any time your children begin sounding unnatural, too loud, or mechanical in their statement responses. Do not let the children get into the habit of responding inappropriately. Such habits, when well established, are very difficult to change.

Presenting Exercises in Which Different Answers are Expected

Many exercises in the program have many correct answers. For example: The teacher says in a Can Do exercise, **"What's one thing you can do with a key?"** or in an Only exercise, **"Say something that is true of only a boat."**

These exercises are to be presented to individual children as indicated in the directions to the teacher. However, the idea is to provide instruction not only for those children who respond but for all members of the group or the class. Therefore, the teacher is usually instructed to have the entire group repeat an individual child's answer.

Follow these general rules when presenting exercises that have a variety of possible answers:

1. Carefully evaluate the student's response.

2. Repeat a correct response so that every member of the group hears it.

3. Ask the group whether or not the response is acceptable.

a. If it is acceptable, have the group repeat it. For example: a teacher is teaching an Only exercise presenting a picture of a shoe and a shirt. **"Bill, say something that is true of only the shoe."**

   Bill says, *"It has shoelaces."*

   Teacher repeats **"It has shoelaces,"** and then says, **"Everybody, look at the picture. Is that true of only the shoe?"**

The children respond, *"Yes."*

b. If it is not acceptable, give the child feedback about the error.

    For example, the teacher is teaching an Only exercise presenting a picture of a boat, a bike and an airplane. The teacher says, **"Janet, say something that is true of only a boat."**

    Janet responds: *"It has a motor."*

    The teacher repeats: **"It has a motor. Everybody, is that true of only a boat? Look at the picture. Name other things 'It has a motor' is true of."**

The children respond, *"An airplane."*

    The teacher: **"Janet, you must name something that is true of only a boat, not a boat and an airplane. Try again."**

    Janet: *"It goes in the water."*

Then the teacher goes through the procedure outlined in step a.

Language Concepts Strand

OVERVIEW

The **Language Concepts** strand teaches children the words, concepts, and statements important to both spoken and written language. This strand emphasizes language as a means of describing the world and as a tool for thinking and solving problems. This language can be described as the language of learning and instruction.

THE FOUNDATION FOR SCHOOL SUCCESS

Language is the underpinning of school success. The content of the Language Concepts strand is based on analyses of what children need in order to do well in school; that is, the words, concepts, and sentence structures they need to understand the content of their school textbooks and other instructional materials. The Language Concepts strand presents vocabulary, background, and knowledge-building exercises, as well as statement analysis, questioning, and definitions exercises. These activities prepare children for the literal and inferential comprehension of the books and other materials they will read both in and out of school.

ORAL LANGUAGE AND READING COMPREHENSION

If children do not understand something that is presented in oral language, it is highly unlikely they will understand the same information presented in written language. In other words, children must have a solid language understanding of what is to be read before they read it. Certainly, children learn new words, new information, and new ideas from reading; however, for this to happen, a language foundation that permits such learning must be in place.

Children in the elementary grades who have little or no trouble comprehending what they read understand commonly–used vocabulary, sentence forms, and instructions used in their textbooks, workbooks, and library books. They make inferences easily because they are practiced in describing the world, following and giving directions, and asking and answering questions. They are good at connecting the content of what they are reading to knowledge they already possess. These children are also good at logical thinking—they understand deductions and the conclusions that follow from key facts. They know how to apply this knowledge in different situations.

FOLLOWING DIRECTIONS AND "FIGURING OUT"

Children who don't have a solid language foundation frequently don't understand the meaning of many of the words their teachers use as they explain new ideas. They often have trouble following the directions that appear in their textbooks and workbooks. They typically have other problems related to language as well: they are not able to retell stories and accounts accurately; they lack much of the general information other children possess; and they have trouble with the logical "figuring out" aspects of language, for example, with true-false concepts, the classification of objects and "if-then" reasoning.

For such children, the teaching of Language Arts can mean the difference between success and failure in learning to read well and doing well in the academic subjects they will encounter in school.

DEVELOPMENT OF TRACKS

Within the Language Concepts strand are different "tracks." Each track develops a particular area of knowledge. The scope and sequence chart on pages 2–3 shows the tracks for the Language Concepts Strand and shows the lesson range on which exercises from each track appear in daily lessons.

For instance, the first track is Actions. It starts in lesson 5 and continues through lesson 78. Classification exercises begin in lesson 1 and appear in most lessons throughout the program.

Following is specific information about what each track teaches.

ACTIONS

The actions track starts in lesson 5 and continues throughout the program. The first exercise in most lessons is an action routine. Routines consist of directions for children to perform specific actions, and questions and instructions that require them to describe what they did, are doing, or will do.

The primary purpose of the action routines is to reinforce and review concepts in an enjoyable routine. The concepts presented include many that were taught in the kindergarten level, such as prepositions; tense; some, all, none; same, different; and, or; and pronouns.

New concepts are sometimes introduced through action exercises.

The objectives of the action routines are:

1. To provide the children with practice that does not smack of drill. Action exercises are fun.

2. To promote facility in the use of specific concept words.

3. To induce facility in saying a variety of statements, applied to both new and familiar settings.

4. To provide you with immediate feedback about the children's performance. If they don't understand the instructions for performing an action, you are able to identify the problem immediately.

This is the first Actions routine, from lesson 5:

EXERCISE 1

ACTIONS

1. Let's play some action games.
- Everybody, you're going to hold up your foot and touch your ears at the same time. Get ready. (Signal.) ✔
- What are you doing? (Signal.) *Holding up my foot and touching my ears.*

2. Say the whole thing. Get ready. (Signal.) *I am holding up my foot and touching my ears.*
- (Repeat step 2 until firm.)

3. Everybody, you're going to touch your chin and hold up your feet. Get ready. (Signal.) ✔
- What are you doing? (Signal.) *Touching my chin and holding up my feet.*

4. Say the whole thing. Get ready. (Signal.) *I am touching my chin and holding up my feet.*
- (Repeat step 3 until firm.)

5. Here's another game. I'm going to do something. See if you can figure out what I'm going to do.

6. Listen: I'm going to shake my head or shake my foot or wave.
- What am I going to do? (Signal.) *Shake your head or shake your foot or wave.*

7. (Repeat step 6 until firm.)

8. Yes, I'm going to shake my head or shake my foot or wave.
- Am I going to wave? (Signal.) *Maybe.*
- Am I going to shake my foot? (Signal.) *Maybe.*
- Am I going to shake my arm? (Signal.) *No.*
- Am I going to shake my head? (Signal.) *Maybe.*

9. Here I go. (Shake your head.)
- Did I shake my head? (Signal.) *Yes.*

- Did I wave? (Signal.) *No.*
- Did I shake my foot? (Signal.) *No.*
10. (Repeat steps 8 and 9 until firm.)

Teaching Notes

Keep your pacing brisk—say your lines quickly. A brisk pace is critical with all the action tasks.

Do not allow the children to lead you. If you do not require them to respond on signal, you will find yourself slowing the pace of the task, waiting for each child to perform an action before presenting the next instruction.

In step 1, after giving the instruction, pause only long enough for the children to perform the action. Then immediately ask the question, What are you doing?

Always make sure that the children are performing the action while they are answering the question What are you doing? They must still be performing it when they say the whole thing. Otherwise, the children will have serious problems with past tense actions.

Make sure the children do **not** respond with a complete statement in step 1. They should say *Holding up my foot and touching my and ears* **not** *I am holding up my foot and touching my ears.* If necessary, lead them through this response several times.

In step 2, lead the children through the statement as many times as necessary so that they can make the statement without your help. You may have to repeat the statement several times.

Do not proceed to steps 5–7, until the children have mastered steps 1–4. Make sure the children are responding together and on signal to all steps of this task on the first day it is presented.

To Correct

If a child does not follow your instruction correctly, point to a child who has and say, Look, John is holding up his foot and touching his ears. If the child still does not perform the action, help him. For example, take his hands and move them to his ears.

Model the question and correct answer in steps 1 and 2, and steps 3 and 4. If the children respond with a complete statement in steps 1 and 3, repeat the pairs of steps until the children respond without error.

Correct errors in a perfunctory manner and then return to the beginning of the section in which the error occurred.

If the children are hesitant to respond or are being led by some of the group, return to the beginning of the series. Give the instruction, pause two seconds, then give a very precise signal. Repeat until all the children are initiating the responses, and are responding on signal.

In this format from lesson 8, the children play a game. They are to respond only if the teacher does exactly the action specified in the first part of the rule. If the teacher does anything else, they are to do nothing.

EXERCISE 1

ACTIONS

1. We're going to learn a rule and play some games.
2. Listen to this rule: **If the teacher touches the floor, say "yes."**
   - Listen again. **If the teacher touches the floor, say "yes."**
   - Everybody, say the rule. Get ready. (Signal.) *If the teacher touches the floor, say yes.*
3. (Repeat step 2 until firm.)
4. Tell me, what are you going to say if I touch the floor? (Signal.) *Yes.*

- Are you going to say **yes** if I touch the floor? (Signal.) *Yes.*
- Are you going to say **yes** if I touch my head? (Signal.) *No.*
- Are you going to say **yes** if I say *"Touch the floor"*? (Signal.) *No.*

5. Now we're going to play the game.
6. Let's see if I can fool you. Get ready. (Pause.) (Touch your head.) (Signal.) (The children should not say anything.)
   - Get ready. (Pause.) (Touch the floor.) (Signal.) *Yes.*
   - See if I can fool you this time. Get ready. (Pause.) **Yes.** (Signal.) (The children should not say anything.)
   - Get ready (Pause.) (Touch the floor.) (Signal.) (Children say *yes.*)
7. (Repeat step 6 until firm.)
   - That's the end of the game.

Teaching Notes

In step 2, present the rule as follows: If the teacher touches the floor, say *yes*.

Make sure that all the children can say the rule before leaving step 2.

Present the questions in step 3 quickly.

Present the last part of the exercise, steps 4–7, as a game. Challenge the children. Let them know you would like to fool them.

To Correct

If the children have trouble saying the rule, repeat the model, lead, and test procedure specified in step 2.

If the children make errors in step 4, correct them and return to the beginning of the step. Then do the entire task again.

CLASSIFICATION

The classification track starts in lesson 1 and continues throughout the program. The classification track has a number of objectives, each of which is important for later in the program. These include:

1. Teaching the names of common classes, such as furniture and vehicles.

2. Setting the stage for the definitions exercises. A definition is constructed by first naming a class for the object to be defined, then by indicating how it is different from the other members of that class.

3. Teaching the relationship between larger and smaller classes, as follows:
   - An object belongs to a number of classes. For example, a yellow pencil is in the classes of yellow pencils, pencils, writing tools, and tools. A larger class has more kinds of things in it. A small class, such as yellow pencils, has only one kind of thing in it; a large class, such as tools, has many different kinds of things in it—pencils, rulers, pliers, and so on.
   - There is a logical test for determining which of two classes is the larger: The larger class has more kinds of things in it. For example, if all trucks are removed from the class of trucks, nothing is left; if all trucks are removed from the class of vehicles, however, many vehicles are left. Therefore, the class of vehicles has more kinds of things in it than the class of trucks.

4. Showing children a new way that objects are the same. For example, a pair of pliers and a pencil are the same because both are tools.

The first classification exercises in the program review the rules for common classes—containers, vehicles, food, tools, clothing.

Here's the classification exercise from lesson 1:

CLASSIFICATION

Containers

1. This is the first language lesson. When we do language lessons, you're going to talk. You're going to name things and learn about things like opposites and rules. You'll learn facts about places and things. You'll learn about the calendar, difficult words, and a lot of other things. Remember to follow my directions and work hard.
   - Let's start with a rule for containers.
2. Listen: If it's made to hold things, it's a container.
   - Say the rule. Get ready. (Signal.) *If it's made to hold things, it's a container.*
   - Again. Say the rule. Get ready. (Signal.) *If it's made to hold things, it's a container.*
   - (Repeat step 2 until firm.)
3. Listen: If something is made to hold things, it is a container. If something is not made to hold things, it is not a container.
4. A box is made to hold things, so what do you know about a box? (Signal.) *It's a container.*
   - A cup is made to hold things, so what do you know about a cup? (Signal.) *It's a container.*
   - A basket is made to hold things, so what do you know about a basket?(Signal.) *It's a container.*
   - A suitcase is made to hold things, so what do you know about a suitcase? (Signal.) *It's a container.*
   - Is a knife is made to hold things? (Signal.) *No.*
   - So what do you know about a knife? (Signal.) *It's not a container.*
5. I'll name some things. You tell me if they are containers.
   - Listen: a log. Tell me: container or not container. (Signal.) *Not container.*

- Listen: a bike. Tell me. (Signal.) *Not container.*
- Listen: a cabinet. Tell me. (Signal.) *Container.*
- Listen: a jar. Tell me. (Signal.) *Container.*
- Listen: a pencil. Tell me. (Signal.) *Not container.*

Teaching Notes

In step 2, you present a rule for containers—**if it's made to hold things, it's a container.** Children learned this rule in the Kindergarten level.

In step 4, you provide children with information they need to classify objects as containers.

Require solid responses from the children. In step 2, they should say the rule correctly. If you're not sure of how firm they are in saying the rule, call on individual children after you direct the group to repeat the rule. In step 4, they are applying the rule about containers. If they make mistakes, correct by referring to the rule for containers. For instance, A suitcase is made to hold things, so what do you know about a suitcase? If children say, *It's a suitcase,* remind them of the rule: Listen, if it's made to hold things, it's a **container.** A suitcase it made to hold things. So a suitcase is a **container.** Then repeat the wording for the question the children missed: Listen, a suitcase is made to hold things, so what do you know about a suitcase?

It's important for the children to hear how they should go about figuring out the answer to the questions you ask. Practice starting with a rule and giving information and drawing conclusions about whether the thing is a container. If it's made to hold things, it's a **container.** A box is made to hold things. So a box is a **container.**

Here are the rules for the classes children learned in the Kindergarten level:

If it is made to take you places, it is a **vehicle.**

If you can eat it, then it's **food.**

If you put things in it, it's a **container.**

If you can wear it, it's **clothing.**

If it has walls and roof, it's a **building.**

If it grows in the ground, it is a **plant.**

If it helps you do work, it's a **tool.**

Children review these rules through lesson 13. Here's the review exercise from lesson 13:

EXERCISE 1

CLASSIFICATION

1. I'm going to name some objects. Tell me a class these objects are in. (Accept all reasonable responses, but then suggest the response given.)
2. Listen: glass, suitcase, purse, box, bottle. Everybody, what class? (Signal.) *Containers.*
   Yes, containers.
   • Listen: plane, train, bus, car, boat. Everybody, what class? (Signal.) *Vehicles.*
   Yes, vehicles.
   • Listen: saw, rake, screwdriver, pliers, ax. Everybody, what class? (Signal.) *Tools.*
   Yes, tools.
   • Listen: bread, burgers, butter, beans. Everybody, what class? (Signal.) *Food.*
   Yes, food.
3. (Repeat step 2 until firm.)
4. I'm going to name a class. See how many objects you can name in that class. Listen: containers. (Call on individual children. Accept all reasonable responses.)
   • I'm going to name another class. See how many objects you can name in that class. Listen: vehicles. (Call on individual children. Accept all reasonable responses.)

   • I'm going to name another class. See how many objects you can name in that class. Listen: tools. (Call on individual children. Accept all reasonable responses.)

Teaching Notes

For this exercise, you name different objects. Children name the class for all the objects. Make sure that children's responses are firm on the classes. If they have a good idea of the objects that are in a class like vehicles, they will be in a good position to learn the new classification operations scheduled for Grade 1 Language Arts.

Starting in lesson 21, they start learning about bigger classes and smaller classes. The test for the size of a class is the different kinds of things that are in the class. A class with more kinds of things in it is bigger than a class with fewer kinds of things in it.

Here's the exercise that introduces bigger-smaller class in lesson 21:

EXERCISE 6

CLASSIFICATION

1. You're going to learn about bigger classes and smaller classes.
   • Here's the rule: The bigger class has more kinds of things in it.
   • Everybody, say that rule. Get ready. (Signal.) *The bigger class has more kinds of things in it.*
2. Listen to these classes: children, girls, baby girls.
   • Everybody, say those three classes. Get ready. (Signal.) *Children, girls, baby girls.*
3. The biggest class is children. It has boys in it. It has girls in it, and it has baby girls in it. What's the biggest class? (Signal.) *Children.*
   • Are there girls in that class? (Signal.) *Yes.*
   • Are there baby girls in that class? (Signal.) *Yes.*
   • Are there boys in that class? (Signal.) *Yes.*

- Say the three classes again. Get ready. (Signal.) *Children, girls, baby girls.*
- Which class is the biggest? (Signal.) *Children.*
  Yes, the biggest class is children.
4. The next biggest class is girls. It has girls and baby girls in it, but it doesn't have boys in it.
- Say the three classes again. Get ready. (Signal.) *Children, girls, baby girls.*
- Which class is the biggest? (Signal.) *Children.*
- Which class is the next biggest? (Signal.) *Girls.*
- Are there girls in that class? (Signal.) *Yes.*
- Are there baby girls in that class? (Signal.) *Yes.*
- Are there boys in that class? (Signal.) *No.*
5. The smallest class is baby girls. It has only baby girls in it, not older girls or any boys.
6. I'll tell you what is in a class. You tell me which class it is.
- Listen: This class has boys and girls and baby girls. Which class is that? (Signal.) *Children.*
- Listen: This class has only baby girls in it. What class is that? (Signal.) *Baby girls.*
- Listen: This class has girls and baby girls in it. But it doesn't have any boys in it. Which class is that? (Signal.) *Girls.*
7. (Repeat step 6 until firm.)

Teaching Notes

These are nested classes, which means that everything inside the smallest class is in the middle-sized class and inside the biggest class. Some children have trouble learning the structure, but if you bring them to a solid criterion of mastery on the first few appearances of the bigger-class exercises, they'll catch on. The program provides for children lots of practice in applying what they learn about these classes.

The strategy for presenting first exercises is to make sure that children's responses are firm by the end of the exercise. They are able to say the rule for bigger classes and are able to apply it to examples that you name. In step 1, children say the rule for bigger classes—make sure that children are very firm on saying the rule before you move on to step 2.

In step 2, you name three classes—children, girls, baby girls. At different points in the exercise, you call on the children to name these three classes. If children tend to produce weak responses, tell them the three classes and go back to the beginning of step 2 and repeat until children's responses are firm.

Step 4 is the most critical step in the exercise. For children to understand how larger classes work, they must know that the larger classes have more kinds of things in them. If children's responses are particularly weak on this step, have the children repeat the descriptions for what is in each class and then tell the name for that class.

Make sure that by the time you have finished the exercise, the children's responses are reasonably firm on the contents of the three classes.

Through lesson 36, children continue to work on different variations of this exercise with different classes they have learned. By lesson 36, they have an understanding that the classes they have learned can be broken down into smaller classes. The class of vehicles, for instance, includes the class of cars, and the class of cars includes the class of red cars.

In lesson 38, children learn more about these nested classes. They learn that the smaller classes they have dealt with can be broken down into even smaller classes. And they learn a test for whether a class is bigger than another class. This test is "logical subtraction." We can show that the class of mashed potatoes is smaller than the class of potatoes by removing mashed potatoes from the class of potatoes. If nothing remains, the classes are the same size. But if other types of potatoes remain, the class of mashed potatoes is smaller than the class of potatoes.

Here's the exercise from lesson 38:

EXERCISE 1

CLASSIFICATION

1. We're going to talk about classes.
2. If we took all potatoes from the class of food, would there be any kinds of food left? (Signal.) *Yes.*
- Name some kinds of food that would be left. (Call on individual children. Praise appropriate responses.)
3. The class of potatoes is made up of many kinds of potatoes in the class of potatoes. Listen: mashed potatoes, boiled potatoes.
- You name some kinds of potatoes in the class of potatoes. (Call on individual children. Praise reasonable answers, such as: fried potatoes, scalloped potatoes, baked potatoes.)
4. Think about this. If we took all the mashed potatoes from the class of potatoes, would there be any potatoes left? (Signal.) *Yes.*
- Name some kinds of potatoes that would be left. (Call on individual children. Praise all acceptable answers: that is, any kind of potato except mashed potatoes.)
5. Yes, if we took all the mashed potatoes from the class of potatoes, there would still be potatoes left. So which class is bigger, the class of mashed potatoes or the class of potatoes? (Signal.) *The class of potatoes.*
- How do you know? (Signal.) *The class of potatoes has more kinds of things in it.*
6. Think big. Which class is bigger, the class of potatoes or the class of food? (Signal.) *The class of food.*
- Think big. Which class is bigger, the class of potatoes or the class of mashed potatoes? (Signal.) *The class of potatoes.*

Teaching Notes

The most crucial part of the exercise is step 5. You ask children how they know the class of potatoes is bigger than the class of mashed potatoes. Children may not recite the exact answer shown *The class of potatoes has more kinds of things in it*, but children are to express this idea. You can lead them by asking additional questions. When we take all the mashed potatoes from the class of potatoes is there anything left? . . . What's left? . . . That tells why the class of potatoes is larger than the class of mashed potatoes. Call on individual children to tell how they know that the class of potatoes is bigger than the class of mashed potatoes. Praise children who give good answers. Prompt those who don't and call on them again.

Children do variations of this exercise and the basic exercise. They also do worksheet activities that involve larger-smaller classes starting with lesson 83. The work provides children with the basic rules about grouping things in different ways.

WORD SKILLS

There are a number of specific things children can do with words if they have been taught the needed skills. The tracks in this group are **opposites, definitions, descriptions, synonyms,** and **contractions.** In these tracks, children learn the skills needed to

1. name and recognize pairs of words that are opposites;
2. define a word—first by naming a class for the things being defined, then by indicating characteristics of the things being defined that are true of only those things;
3. identify objects that are described through clues;
4. name and recognize synonyms;
5. form contractions using the correct pronoun and verb forms.

OPPOSITES

The opposites track begins with a review of opposites taught in the Kindergarten level. These opposites are reviewed through lesson 20.

Starting at lesson 21, new opposite pairs are added to the set the children work with. First, each new opposite pair is presented in an introduction exercise. Next, an exercise gives the children practice in using opposites. Finally, the opposite pairs are reviewed.

Following is a list of the opposite pairs reviewed and taught in Grade 1 Language Arts.

Opposites	Lesson Introduced (or reviewed)
dry/wet, fat/skinny, small/big, young/old, full/empty, long/short	1
hotter/colder	3
short/tall	11
big/little	17
fast/slow	21
happy/sad	22
awake/asleep	23
narrow/wide	25
noisy/quiet	26
difficult/easy, winning/losing	39
crying/laughing	40
pushing/pulling, shiny/dull, dangerous/safe, raw/cooked	55
smooth/rough, shallow/deep	56
before/after, early/late, start/finish	59
under/over, wild/tame	62
shut/open	63
throwing/catching	66
in front of/in back of	67
feeling sick/feeling well	96
clean/dirty	98
far/near	100
quickly/slowly	106
bad/good	121
light/dark	126
strong/weak	130

Starting in lesson 1, children review the structure of opposites. **If something is wet, we know that it is not dry. If something is tall, we know that it is not short.**
Here's the review from lesson 1:

EXERCISE 2

OPPOSITES

1. Some words let you figure out things. Those are words like dry, skinny, full, young, long.
   - If something is dry, it is not wet.
   - If something is fat, it is not skinny.
   - If something is small, it is not big.
   - If something is young, it is not old.
   - If something is full, it is not empty.
   - If something is long, it is not short.
2. Your turn. If something is dry, what else do you know about it? (Signal.) *It is not wet.*
   - If something is fat, what else do you know about it? (Signal.) *It is not skinny.*
   - If something is small, what else do you know about it? (Signal.) *It is not big.*
   - If something is young, what else do you know about it? (Signal.) *It is not old.*
   - If something is full, what else do you know about it? (Signal.) *It is not empty.*
   - If something is long, what else do you know about it? (Signal.) *It is not short.*
3. (Repeat step 2 until firm.)
4. Listen: I'm thinking of a chicken that is skinny. What else do you know about it? (Signal.) *It is not fat.*
   - Listen: I'm thinking of a leaf that is wet. What else do you know about it? (Signal.) *It is not dry.*
   - Listen: I'm thinking of a rope that is long. What else do you know about it? (Signal.) *It is not short.*
   - Say the whole thing about the rope. Get ready. (Signal.) *The rope is not short.* Yes, the rope is not short.
   - Listen: I'm thinking of a jug that is empty. What else do you know about it? Get ready. (Signal.) *It is not full.*

- Say the whole thing about the jug. Get ready. (Signal.) *The jug is not full.*
- Listen: I'm thinking of a duck that is young. What else do you know about it? (Signal.) *It is not old.*
- Say the whole thing about the duck. Get ready. (Signal.) *The duck is not old.*

Teaching Notes

In step 1, you review the relationship between pairs of different opposites. In step 2, you test children on this relationship. In step 4, you apply this relationship to concrete situations. Step 2 is the critical step in this exercise. Repeat the step if children's responses are not firm. Once they are firm on this step, children should have no trouble applying the rules to the concrete examples described in step 4.

In lesson 17, children review the word **opposite** and identify pairs of opposites. Here's the exercise:

EXERCISE 7

OPPOSITES

1. Some words are opposites. Here are opposites: long and short. They are opposites because if something is long, you know it can't be short.
- You know the opposite of big. What's the opposite of big? (Signal.) *Small.*
- Here's another pair of opposites: big and little.
- From now on, what will you say for the opposite of big? (Signal.) *Little.*
- Here's another pair of opposites: young and old.
2. Your turn. What are young and old? (Signal.) *Opposites.*
- What are big and little? (Signal.) *Opposites.*
- What are long and short? (Signal.) *Opposites.*

- Who can name another pair of opposites? (Call on individual children. Ideas: wet and dry; fat and skinny; tall and short; full and empty.)
3. I'll say words. You tell me the opposite.
- Listen: empty. What's the opposite of empty? (Signal.) *Full.*
- Yes, full is the opposite of . . . (Signal.) *empty.*
- Say the whole thing about full. Get ready. (Signal.) *Full is the opposite of empty.*
- Listen: old. What's the opposite of old? (Signal.) *Young.*
- Say the whole thing about young. Get ready. (Signal.) *Young is the opposite of old.*
- Listen: tall. What's the opposite of tall? (Signal.) *Short.*
- Say the whole thing about short. Get ready. (Signal.) *Short is the opposite of tall.*
4. (Repeat step 3 until firm.)

Teaching Notes

Step 3 is the critical step. If children perform well on this step, you know that they understand that opposites occur in pairs and that they are called opposites. Make sure children's responses are firm on step c. In later lessons, children respond to descriptions that use the word **opposite.**

Here's the exercise from lesson 20:

EXERCISE 4

OPPOSITES

1. Get ready to tell me about opposites.
2. I'm thinking of an alligator that is the opposite of dry. So what do you know about it? (Signal.) *It's wet.*
- I'm thinking of an alligator that is the opposite of cold. So what do you know about it? (Signal.) *It's hot.*
- I'm thinking of an alligator that is the opposite of old. So what do you know about it? (Signal.) *It's young.*

- I'm thinking of an alligator that is the opposite of skinny. So what do you know about it? (Signal.) *It's fat.*
- I'm thinking of an alligator that is the opposite of empty. So what do you know about it? (Signal.) *It's full.*
3. (Repeat step 2 until firm.)

Teaching Notes

This type of exercise is like some of the earlier review exercises except that it uses the word opposite. Instead of saying, for instance, I'm thinking of something that is not full, you say, I'm thinking of something that is the **opposite** of full.

New pairs of opposites are introduced beginning with lesson 21. Some of the children will know some of the opposites; however, even though the children may know some of the opposite words, they may not have a clear idea that the word is paired with another word and that the pair functions as opposites.

Here's the exercise from lesson 21:

EXERCISE 5

| OPPOSITES |

1. I'll tell you about some new opposites.
- Listen. The opposite of fast is slow. What's the opposite of fast? (Signal.) *Slow.*
- What's the opposite of slow? (Signal.) *Fast.*
2. Get ready to tell me about opposites.
- I'm thinking of a duck that is the opposite of dry. So what do you know about it? (Signal.) *It's wet.*
- I'm thinking of a duck that is the opposite of tall. So what do you know about it? (Signal.) *It's short.*
- I'm thinking of a duck that is the opposite of slow. So what do you know about it? (Signal.) *It's fast.*
- I'm thinking of a duck that is the opposite of cold. So what do you know about it? (Signal.) *It's hot.*

- I'm thinking of a duck that is the opposite of young. So what do you know about it? (Signal.) *It's old.*
- I'm thinking of a duck that is the opposite of skinny. So what do you know about it? (Signal.) *It's fat.*
3. (Repeat step 2 until firm.)

Teaching Notes

In step 1, you present the new pair of opposites. In step 2, you review that pair in the context of familiar opposites.
You should be able to present this material quite fast, and the children should tend to not make any mistakes.
Starting with lesson 46, children say statements that use opposites.

Here's the exercise from lesson 46:

EXERCISE 6

| OPPOSITES |

1. Let's make up statements with the opposite word.
2. Listen. The boy is **laughing.** Say that statement. (Signal.) *The boy is laughing.*
3. Now say a statement with the opposite of **laughing.** Get ready. (Signal.) *The boy is crying.*
4. (Repeat steps b and c until firm.)
5. Listen. The door is **narrow.** Say that statement Get ready. (Signal.) *The door is narrow.*
6. Now say a statement with the opposite of **narrow.** Get ready. (Signal.) *The door is wide.*
7. (Repeat steps 5 and 6 until firm.)

Teaching Notes

Although the exercise is short, it presents important practice—creating a sentence that is parallel to the sentence you give but that has a specified opposite word, which gives the sentence the opposite meaning of the original. This extension of opposites to sentences seems very obvious but it is not always that obvious to the children. Make sure that they are firm on saying the opposite sentences.

DEFINITIONS

Children receive some practice in constructing definitions, starting in lesson 41. The goal of the instruction is to acquaint children with how definitions give word meanings. They use a two-step operation. First, they identify a class for the word that is being defined. Next, they tell something about what is being defined that is true only of that object. For instance, to define gold, the class for the object is identified—metal. Then the definition says things about gold that cannot be said about other metals: it is valuable, has a gold color, and does not rust or tarnish. Here's the definitions exercise from lesson 41:

EXERCISE 1

DEFINITIONS

1. We're going to make up a definition for corn.
- First we name a class. Then we say something that is true of only corn. Remember, first we name a class. What do we do first when we make up a definition? (Signal.) *Name a class.*
- Next we say something that is true of only corn.
- What do we do next? (Signal.) *Say something that is true of only corn.*
2. (Repeat step 1 until firm.)
3. Once more. Everybody, what do we do first? (Signal.) *Name a class.*
- What do we do next? (Signal.) *Say something that is true of only corn.*
4. (Repeat step 3 until firm.)
5. Now let's make up a definition. Everybody, what do we do first? (Signal.) *Name a class.*

- Name a class for **corn.** (Call on individual children. Accept reasonable responses but use: *food or plant.*)
  Yes, corn is a food or corn is a plant.
- We named a class. Now what do we do? (Signal.) *Say something that is true of only corn.*
- Yes, now say something that is true of only corn. (Call on one or two children. Accept all reasonable responses, but use: *It grows on ears.*)
  Yes, it grows on ears.
6. I'll say the definition for **corn:** Corn is food that grows on ears.
7. Your turn. Say the definition for **corn.** Get ready. (Signal.) *Corn is food that grows on ears.*
- (Repeat step 7 until firm.)
8. We're going to make up a definition for **tree.** Everybody, what do we do first? (Signal.) *Name a class.*
- Name a class for **tree.** Get ready. (Signal.) *Plants.*
  Yes, a tree is a plant.
- We named a class. Now what do we do? (Signal.) *Say something that is true of only a tree.*
- Yes, now say something that is true of only a tree. (Call on one or two children. Accept all reasonable responses, but use: *It has leaves, branches, and a trunk.*)
  Yes, it has leaves, branches, and a trunk.
9. Everybody, now say the definition for **tree.** Get ready. (Signal.) *A tree is a plant that has leaves, branches, and a trunk.*
- (Repeat step 9 until firm.)
10. Let's see if you remember these definitions.
- Everybody, say the definition for **corn.** Get ready. (Signal.) *Corn is food that grows on ears.*
- Everybody, say the definition for **tree.** Get ready. (Signal.) *A tree is a plant that has leaves, branches, and a trunk.*

Teaching Notes

Rehearse this exercise before you present it. Make sure you know exactly what you expect the children to do at each step. First you tell them the steps for creating a definition. In step 3, you ask them What do we do first? and What do we do next? Make sure that children are very firm on their responses. In step 5, they will apply this procedure to defining corn.

First, children name a class for corn. They may name a class that is too large, such as *object*. Tell them that they need a smaller class. Don't accept any classes unless they are true for all examples of corn. For instance, a child may say that *It's something in the kitchen.* Don't accept that class. *A child may say that It is a material.* Don't accept that class. A child may say *It grows on a farm.* That class is probably acceptable (even though there may be wild corn, which is not included in the class).

Children may also have trouble saying something that is true of only corn. They may say things like, *It's yellow; It grows; It's tall* or similar things that are true of other things besides corn. Acknowledge that what they say is true of corn, but that is true of other things as well. For example, if children say that *Corn is yellow*, say, Yes, it's yellow. But it's not the only food that is yellow. Who can name some other foods that are yellow? . . .*(banana, squash)*

If children have a lot of trouble, tell them I'll say things that are true of corn. You'll tell me if they are true of only corn. It's food that grows on a farm . . . It's food that is tall . . . It's food that is good to eat . . . It's food that's yellow . . . It's food that grows on ears.

In step 7, children say that definition for corn: *Corn is food that grows on ears.* Make sure that children are firm on saying the definition. After children have completed the definition of corn, have them repeat the definition and possibly say the parts of the definition. Say the part of the definition that tells the class for corn.

Say the part of the definition that tells something that is true of only corn. Repeat the definition until children's responses are firm. In step 8, children repeat the steps as they create a definition for tree. In lessons 42 and 43, children practice making up definitions for other common objects (spider, elephant, bird, hammer).

SYNONYMS

Grade 1 Language Arts teaches the following synonym pairs:

Synonyms	Lesson Introduced
shut, close	77
skinny, thin	77
under, below	79
large, big	80
little, small	80
yell, shout	81
above, over	81
well, healthy	89
crying, weeping	90
fast, quick(ly)	97
near, close to	110
hard, difficult	110
bright, shiny	111
same, alike	115
end, finish	116

The work with synonyms begins in lesson 77 and continues to the end of the level. The only difference between "synonyms" and the funny words (such as zatch in lesson 77) that are presented through the description exercises is that synonyms are established words that mean the same thing (not a made up word that means the same thing as an established word). The work with descriptions sets the stage for synonyms.

Children sometimes have trouble distinguishing between opposites and synonyms. For this reason, synonyms are not introduced until the children have practiced opposites for many lessons.

The first synonyms are introduced as words that **mean the same thing.** Sentence tasks, reviews, and stories are part of each cycle.

The exercise in lesson 77 introduces the word *synonyms* and gives a definition. Here's the exercise:

EXERCISE 2

SYNONYMS

1. We're going to learn what **synonym** means.
2. Synonym. Say that. (Signal.) *Synonym.*
   • (Repeat until firm.)
3. Listen to the rule. A synonym is a word that means the same thing as another word.
4. Listen again: A synonym is a word that means the same thing as another word. Let's say that. Get ready. (Respond with the children.) *A synonym is a word that means the same thing as another word.*
5. All by yourselves. Say the rule. Get ready. (Signal.) *A synonym is a word that means the same thing as another word.*
6. (Repeat steps 4 and 5 until firm.)
7. What do we call a word that means the same thing as another word? (Signal.) *A synonym.*
   • Say the rule. Get ready. (Signal.) *A synonym is a word that means the same thing as another word.*

Teaching Notes

Repeat step 2 until the children say **synonym** correctly. This is a difficult word for some children so you may have to repeat this step several times.

The rule in step 4 may require a number (four or more) of repetitions before the children can say it. To make it easier for the children to remember the rule, phrase it in a sing-song way, stressing the words **same thing.**

A synonym is a word that means the **same thing** as another word.

• Use the individual tests as an indicator of whether the rule should be repeated. If more than one child has trouble, repeat the exercise from the beginning. Then repeat the individual tests.

To Correct

If the children have trouble with the rule

1. Model the first part of the rule:
   A synonym is a word that means . . .
2. Say this part of the rule with the children. (Lead)
3. Have them say this part of the rule without help from you. (Test)
4. Model the entire rule: A synonym is a word that means the same thing as another word.

If the children have trouble with any words in the second part of the rule, have them say the troublesome words before you repeat the entire rule.

In lesson 78, children apply what they have learned about synonyms by making up statements that mean the same thing. These statements have the same words except for the pair of synonyms. Because the synonyms mean the same thing, the sentences mean the same thing.

Here's the exercise from lesson 78:

EXERCISE 4

SYNONYMS

1. We're going to talk about synonyms.
2. Remember the rule: A synonym is a word that means the same thing as another word. Say that. Get ready. (Signal.) *A synonym is a word that means the same thing as another word.*
   • (Repeat step 2 until firm.)

3. What's a word that means the same thing as another word? (Signal.) *A synonym.*

• Say the rule. Get ready. (Signal.) *A synonym is a word that means the same thing as another word.*

4. Let's make up statements that mean the same thing as other statements.

5. Listen. The book is thin. Say that. (Signal.) *The book is thin.*

6. Here's the statement that has a synonym: the book is skinny. Say that. (Signal.) *The book is skinny.*

7. I'll say one of the statements. You say the statement that has a synonym. My turn: The book is thin. Your turn. (Signal.) *The book is skinny.*

8. (Repeat steps 5 through 8 until firm.)

9. Here's another one.

10. Listen. Please close the window. Say that. (Signal.) *Please close the window.*

11. Here's a statement that has a synonym: Please shut the window. Say that. (Signal.) *Please shut the window.*

12. I'll say one of the statements. You say the statement that has a synonym. My turn: Please close the window. Your turn. (Signal.) *Please shut the window.*

13. (Repeat steps 11 and 12 until firm.)

Teaching Notes

Present the activity as a game. Read as if you enjoy this activity. Make sure that children are firm in saying the sentences with the synonyms.

If children say opposites instead of synonyms, tell them what they did and repeat the task. Return to it later to make sure that children's responses are firm.

To Correct

If children make up statements that contain opposites follow this correction:

1. You made up a statement with the opposite for **thin.** I want a statement with the synonym for **thin.** The synonym for thin is the word that means the same thing as **thin.** Everybody, what word is that? The children respond *Skinny.*

2. Repeat the step in which the mistake occurred.

The last type of synonym exercise begins in lesson 85. You present a story containing familiar words. The children name the synonyms for some of them. Then children say statements with the synonyms.

Here's the exercise from lesson 85:

EXERCISE 1

SYNONYMS

1. I'm going to make up a story. You're going to say the story too, but you are going to use synonyms.

2. There was a boy who was very thin.

• What's a synonym for **thin?** (Signal.) *Skinny.*

• So there was a boy who was very . . . (Signal.) *skinny.*

3. This boy really liked to shout.

• What's a synonym for **shout?** (Signal.) *Yell.*

• So this boy really liked to . . . (Signal.) *yell.*

4. One day he got in the closet and closed the door.

• What's the synonym for **closed?** (Signal.) *Shut.*

• So one day he got in the closet and . . . (Signal.) *shut the door.*

5. Let's do that story one more time and go a little faster.

6. There was a boy who was very thin. Say that. (Signal.) *There was a boy who was very thin.*

- Now say that statement with a synonym for **thin.** Get ready. (Signal.) *There was a boy who was very skinny.*
7. This boy really liked to shout. Say that. (Signal.) *This boy really liked to shout.*
- Now say that statement with a synonym for **shout.** Get ready. (Signal.) *This boy really liked to yell.*
8. One day he got in the closet and closed the door. Say that. (Signal.) *One day he got in the closet and closed the door.*
- Now say that statement with a synonym for **closed.** Get ready. (Signal.) *One day he got in the closet and shut the door.*

Teaching Notes

The children have been making statements with opposites for some time. Expect them to make mistakes in steps 2 and 3 the first time this exercise appears. One way you can help them is to stress the word **synonym** in your directions and give the children thinking time before signaling them to respond.

CONTRACTIONS

The objectives of this track are:
1. To teach subject-verb agreement.
2. To provide practice with the following contractions:

isn't	wasn't	doesn't	didn't
aren't	weren't	don't	

Here's the exercise from Lesson 120:

EXERCISE 3

CONTRACTIONS

1. It's time for some statements.
2. I'll say a statement about a boy. (Point to a boy.) He **does not** have wings. Now I'll say it a new way. He **doesn't** have wings.
3. Everybody, say the statement the **new** way. Get ready. (Signal.) *He doesn't have wings.*
- (Repeat step 3 until firm.)
4. Listen: You do not have wings. Now I'll say it a new way. You **don't** have wings.
5. Everybody, say the statement the **new** way. Get ready. (Signal.) *You don't have wings.*
- (Repeat step 5 until firm.)
6. Listen: She does not have wings. Now I'll say it a **new** way. She **doesn't** have wings.
7. Everybody, say the statement the **new** way. Get ready. (Signal.) *She doesn't have wings.*
- (Repeat step 7 until firm.)
8. Listen: They do **not have** wings. Now I'll say it a **new** way. They **don't** have wings.
9. Everybody, say the statement the new way. Get ready. (Signal.) *They don't have wings.*
- (Repeat step 9 until firm.)
10. Now let's see how fast you can go.
11. (Point to a boy.) Does he have wings? (Signal.) *No.*
- Say the statement the new way. Get ready. (Signal.) *He doesn't have wings.*
12. (Point to two boys.) Do they have wings? (Signal.) *No.*
- Say the statement the new way. Get ready. (Signal.) *They don't have wings.*
13. (Point to a girl.) Does she have wings? (Signal.) *No.*
- Say the statement the new way. Get ready. (Signal.) *She doesn't have wings.*
14. (Repeat steps 11 through 13 until firm.)

Teaching Notes

The exercise has two parts. In the first part (steps 1–8), the teacher models four statements with **doesn't** and **don't.** In the last part of the exercise, the children produce statements with contractions after answering questions on which the statements are based.

Steps 2 and 3, 4 and 5, 6 and 7, and 8 and 9 are paired statements. Each pair should be paced quickly, with a slight pause between pairs.

Listen carefully for mistakes—doesn't for don't, has for have, and the like.

To Correct

If children say an inappropriate word or words in the statements like *He don't have wings* or *We doesn't have wings:*

1. Say the correct word or words: **Doesn't** or **Don't have.**
2. Everybody, say that.
3. (Present a model of the statement again:) He **doesn't** have wings.
4. Everybody, say that.
5. (Return to the beginning of step 3.)

Use the same correction if children say the sentence without the contraction: *He does not have wings.*

You may have to repeat steps 3 and 4 of the correction quite a few times before all the children will be firm on the statements.

Later exercises introduce new contractions. These exercises present questions. As part of answering the questions, children use contractions.

Here's the exercise from lesson 121:

EXERCISE 4

CONTRACTIONS

1. (Point to a boy.)
- Everybody, is he a boy? (Signal.) *Yes.*
- My turn to say the statement the new way. **He's a boy.**
- Everybody, say the statement the new way. Get ready. (Signal.) *He's a boy.*
2. It's time for some questions and statements.
- (Point to a girl.)
- Everybody, does she have three arms? (Signal.) *No.*
- My turn to say the statement the new way. She **doesn't** have three arms.
- Everybody, say the statement the new way. Get ready. (Signal.) *She doesn't have three arms.*
3. (Point to several children.)
- Everybody, do they have three arms? (Signal.) *No.*
- My turn to say the statement the new way. They **don't** have three arms.
- Everybody, say the statement the new way. Get ready. (Signal.) *They don't have three arms.*
4. Now let's see how fast you can go.
- (Point to a girl.)
- Does she have three arms? (Signal.) *No.*
- Say the statement the new way. Get ready. (Signal.) *She doesn't have three arms.*
5. (Point to several children.)
- Do they have three arms? (Signal.) *No.*
- Say the statement the new way. Get ready. (Signal.) *They don't have three arms.*
6. (Point to a boy.)
- Does he have three arms? (Signal.) *No.*
- Say the statement the new way. Get ready. (Signal.) *He doesn't have three arms.*

Teaching Notes

Expect children to make some mistakes when answering the questions about he or she. In step 4, you ask, Does she have three arms? When children attempt to say the answer the new way, they may say, She don't have three arms.

To correct the mistake, stop the children as soon as you hear the word *don't*.

Call the children's attention to the word **does** in the question you ask. Listen: I asked about does. Does she have three arms? The answer is She doesn't have three arms.

Use a similar correction for the question, Do they have three arms? If children try to use the word doesn't, point out, I didn't ask about does. So you shouldn't tell me about does.

Practice the correction. Make sure that you correct the mistakes that children make. If they make persistent mistakes, review the entire exercise until their responses are firm. You may have to return to the exercise at the beginning of the next language period.

SENTENCE SKILLS

Four tracks comprise this group:

(1) Who–What–When–Where–Why

(2) Questioning Skills

(3) Verb Tense

(4) Statements

The common element of these tracks is that they deal with some of the properties of sentences and set the stage for grammatical analysis.

The first track in the group demonstrates that specific parts of sentences answer the questions **who, what, when, where,** or **why.** For example, the sentence "The dog sat on the fence" provides an answer to the questions, "Where did the dog sit?" "Who sat on the fence?" and "What did the dog do?" The children's facility with these questions is a good indicator of how they will perform in reading comprehension.

The **questioning skills** track gives the children practice in asking questions, discriminating between the question and the answer and between the answer and the answer expressed as a complete statement. The track demonstrates the basic difference between two types of sentences—questions and statements.

The **verb tense** track provides practice in transforming statements in a given tense to statements in other tenses. For example, given a present tense statement, the children transform it to either a past tense statement or a future tense statement.

One major purpose of the **statements** track is to demonstrate that a particular statement is limited in what it tells about an event.

WHO–WHAT–WHEN–WHERE–WHY

The track teaches sentence-analysis and question-answering skills that are basic to reading comprehension. Some children may find the exercise difficult. It is important to teach every exercise carefully and thoroughly.

The exercise in lesson 2 presents sentences that have a part that tells **where** and other sentences that do not tell **where.** The goal of this exercise is to acquaint children with the specific words in the sentence that answer the question where.

Here's the exercise from lesson 2:

EXERCISE 2

WHERE

1. Everybody, put two fingers on your elbow. Get ready. (Signal.) (Wait.) ✔
- **Where** are your fingers? (Signal.) *On my elbow.*
- Put two fingers on your wrist. Get ready. (Signal.) (Wait.) ✔
- **Where** are your fingers? (Signal.) *On my wrist.*
- **Where** were your fingers? (Signal.) *On my elbow.*

- Say the whole thing about where your fingers were. Get ready. (Signal.) *My fingers were on my elbow.*
2. Some statements tell where.
- Listen: My fingers were on my elbow. That statement tells **where.**
- Here are the words that tell **where:** on my elbow.
- Listen to the statement again: My fingers were on my elbow. Does that statement tell **where?** (Signal.) *Yes.*
- Say the words in the statement that tell **where.** Get ready. (Signal.) *On my elbow.*
3. Listen: The car was in the driveway. That statement tells **where.**
- Say the words in the statement that tell **where.** Get ready. (Signal.) *In the driveway.*
- Listen: The book was on the refrigerator. Does that statement tell **where?** (Signal.) *Yes.*
- Say the words in the statement that tell **where.** Get ready. (Signal.) *On the refrigerator.*
- Listen: The dog was under the tree. Does that statement tell **where?** (Signal.) *Yes.*
- Say the words in the statement that tell **where.** Get ready. (Signal.) *Under the tree.*
- Listen: The man was sad. Does that statement tell **where?** (Signal.) *No.*
- That statement does not tell **where.** There are no words in it that tell **where** something was.
- Listen: The dog was sleeping. Does that statement tell **where?** (Signal.) *No.*
- Listen: The cat was next to the garage. Does that statement tell **where?** (Signal.) *Yes.*
- Say the words in the statement that tell **where.** Get ready. (Signal.) *Next to the garage.*
- Listen: The penny was under the dresser. Does that statement tell **where?** (Signal.) *Yes.*
- Say the words in the statement that tell **where.** Get ready. (Signal.) *Under the dresser.*

4. Remember, a statement tells **where** if it has words that tell **where.**

Teaching Notes

In step 1, you ask familiar **where** questions. The children should have no problems in answering these questions. In step 2 you introduce the idea that some statements have a part that tells **where.**

In step 3, you present sentences that have a part that tells where and other sentences that do not tell where. Children identify the parts that tell **where.**

Make sure that the group is able to answer all the questions correctly. You may have to repeat step 3 three or more times before all the children's responses are firm. One of the problems that some children have is that they omit some of the words that tell where. For example, instead of saying, *Under the tree,* they may say *The tree,* or *Under.* Correct the children by telling them the response and then have them repeat the task.

Also, children may not discriminate between sentences that tell where and those that do not. For the sentence, "The man was sad," some children may say that it tells where. Show them how to test the sentence. Listen to the first part of the statement, The man. Does that tell **where?**

Listen to the last part of the statement. Was sad. Does that tell **where?** No part of the statement tells **where,** so the statement does not tell **where.**

Children review parts that tell **where** up through lesson 5. Then they learn about parts that tell **when** after they once more review parts that tell **where.** Here's the part of the exercise in lesson 5 that tells **when.**

3. Listen: Some statements tell **when.** Here are parts that tell **when: yesterday, tomorrow, right now, in a minute, before school, at lunchtime.**
- Here's a statement that tells **when:** We work very hard in the morning. Listen: **When** do we work hard? (Signal.) *In the morning.*

- Say the statement. Get ready. (Signal.) *We work very hard in the morning.*
- Say the words in the statement that tell **when.** Get ready. (Signal.) *In the morning.*
4. New statement: We take a break at lunch time. Listen: **When** do we take a break? (Signal.) *At lunch time.*
- Say the statement. Get ready. (Signal.) *We take a break at lunch time.*
- Say the words in that statement that tell **when.** Get ready. (Signal.) *At lunch time.*
5. New statement: The baby cried at four in the morning. Listen: **When** did the baby cry? (Signal.) *At four in the morning.*
- Say the statement. Get ready. (Signal.) *The baby cried at four in the morning.*
- Say the words in that statement that tell **when.** Get ready. (Signal.) *At four in the morning.*
6. New statement: I do a lot of things before school begins.
- Say the statement. Get ready. (Signal.) *I do a lot of things before school begins.*
- Say the words in that statement that tell **when.** Get ready. (Signal.) *Before school begins.*

Teaching Notes

This exercise does not require the children to discriminate between parts that tell where and parts that tell when. However, they must identify the parts that tell when. Make sure that their responses are firm in steps 4, 5, and 6. In lesson 7, children discriminate between statements that tell where and statements that tell when. In this lesson, children first review statements that tell where. Then they review statements that tell when. Finally, they discriminate between the two types of the statements.

Here's the part of the exercise that requires them to tell whether the statement tells **where** or **when.**

7. I'll say statements. Some will tell **when.** Some will tell **where.**

- Listen: The boat sailed under the bridge. Does that statement tell **where** or tell **when?** (Signal.) *Where.*
- Say the words that tell **where.** Get ready. (Signal.) *Under the bridge.*
8. Listen: The boat sailed in the evening. Does that statement tell **where** or tell **when?** (Signal.) *When.*
- Say the words that tell **when.** Get ready. (Signal.) *In the evening.*
9. Listen: The boat sailed near the shore. Does that statement tell **where** or tell **when?** (Signal.) *Where.*
- Say the words that tell **where.** Get ready. (Signal.) *Near the shore.*
10. Listen: The boat sailed for five days. Does that statement tell **where** or tell **when?** (Signal.) *When.*
- Say the words that tell **when.** Get ready. (Signal.) *For five days.*
11. Listen: The boat sailed during a terrible storm. Does that statement tell **where** or tell **when?** (Signal.) *When.*
- Say the words that tell **when.** Get ready. (Signal.) *During a terrible storm.*
12. Listen: The boat sailed over large waves. Does that statement tell **where** or tell **when?** (Signal.) *Where.*
- Say the words that tell **where.** Get ready. (Signal.) *Over large waves.*

Teaching Notes

If children's responses are quite firm on where and on what they had learned about on lessons 5 through 7, they should not have serious problems with the discrimination. If their responses are not firm, however, they will have problems, particularly if they make mistakes on the preceding practice that lesson 7 provides with where and when statements. If the children start to make "guessing" mistakes on the part above, go on to the next part of the lesson and come back to this part later. Don't try to "drill" the children if they have been working on where and when for more than a few minutes.

Remember to come back to this part and firm responses, starting with the exercise that reviews where and correcting any mistakes students make. Also, if children had made mistakes on the part of the exercise shown above, first model the answers for each statement. Then present the statement to the children the way the script indicates.

In the following lessons, children review where and when. Starting in lesson 20, children are introduced to who. You present sentences that answer questions about **when, where,** and **who.** Here's the exercise:

EXERCISE 6

WHO–WHERE–WHEN

1. I'm going to say sentences that answer a lot of questions. You'll answer the questions.
   - Listen. The boys hiked near the river after school.
   - Listen again. The boys hiked near the river after school.
   - Your turn. Say the sentence. Get ready. (Signal.) *The boys hiked near the river after school.*
   - That sentence has words that tell **who,** words that tell **where,** and words that tell **when.**
2. Listen. The boys hiked near the river after school.
   - Everybody, say that sentence. Get ready. (Signal.) *The boys hiked near the river after school.*
   - Who hiked? (Signal.) *The boys.*
   - When did the boys hike? (Signal.) *After school.*
   - Where did the boys hike? (Signal.) *Near the river.*
3. Everybody, say the whole sentence. Get ready. (Signal.) *The boys hiked near the river after school.*

- Which words tell who hiked? (Signal.) *The boys.*
- Which words tell where they hiked? (Signal.) *Near the river.*
- Which words tell when they hiked? (Signal.) *After school.*
4. (Repeat steps 2 and 3 until firm.)
5. New statement. Seven mice went in the barn last night.
   - Everybody, say the sentence. Get ready. (Signal.) *Seven mice went in the barn last night.*
   - Who was in the barn? (Signal.) *Seven mice.*
   - Where did the seven mice go? (Signal.) *In the barn.*
   - When did the mice go in the barn? (Signal.) *Last night.*
6. Everybody, say the whole sentence. Get ready. (Signal.) *Seven mice went in the barn last night.*
   - Which words tell who went in the barn? (Signal.) *Seven mice.*
   - Which words tell where they went? (Signal.) *In the barn.*
   - Which words tell when they went in the barn? (Signal.) *Last night.*
7. (Repeat steps 5 and 6 until firm.)

Teaching Notes

In step 2 children answer questions about who, where and when. Expect some children to make mistakes on the question **Where** did the boys hike? They will say, *Near the river after school.*

Tell them: You told me about **where** and about **when.** My turn: **Where** did they hike? *Near the river.*

When did they hike there? *After school.*

Your turn: **Where** did they hike?

When did they hike there?

Repeat until firm.

In step 3, you ask the children to identify the words in the sentence that tell **who, where,** and **when.**

Children are often able to answer the questions about who, where, and when but are unable to say the words that tell who, where, or when. To correct mistakes follow these steps:
1. Repeat the sentence.
2. Ask the question about **who, where,** or **when.**
3. Tell students that the words they said to answer the questions are the words that tell **who, where,** or **when.**
For example, you present the statement, The boys hiked near the river after school. Then you ask, Which words tell **where** they hiked? and some of the children don't respond. Correct by saying: Listen. The boys hiked near the river after school. **Where** did the boys hike? The children say *Near the river.* Tell them, Those are the words that tell **where.**
Say the words that tell **where.**
Return to the beginning of step 3 and present the step.

In lesson 27 children answer questions about **what.**
Here's the exercise from lesson 27:

EXERCISE 4

WHO–WHERE–WHEN–WHAT

1. I'm going to say a sentence that answers questions about **who, where, when,** and **what.** You'll answer the questions.
2. Listen. Last night, two birds flew into the nest.
• Listen again. Last night, two birds flew into the nest.
• Your turn. Say the sentence. Get ready. (Signal.) *Last night, two birds flew into the nest.*
• Listen. **Who** flew into the nest? (Signal.) *Two birds.*
• Listen. **What** did the birds do? (Signal.) *Flew into the nest.*
• When did the birds do that? (Signal.) *Last night.*

• **Where** did the birds go? (Signal.) *Into the nest.*
3. Listen again. Last night, two birds flew into the nest.
• Everybody, say the whole sentence. Get ready. (Signal.) *Last night, two birds flew into the nest.*
• Which words tell who? (Signal.) *Two birds.*
• Which word tells what they did? (Signal.) *Flew.*
• Which words tell when? (Signal.) *Last night.*
• Which words tell where? (Signal.) *Into the nest.*
4. (Repeat step 3 until firm.)

Teaching Notes

Children should not have serious problems with **what** questions. They have answered these as part of their action routines. (**What** are you doing?) and as part of their picture-identification routines (**What** color is the dog? **What** kind of animal is next to the dog?). Expect some children to have trouble with step 3. Tell them the correct answers and repeat the step. Repeat the step at a later time if the children's responses are not perfectly firm when you leave the exercise.

In lesson 31 children are introduced to parts that tell **why.** Here's the exercise.

EXERCISE 4

WHO–WHEN–WHAT–WHY

1. I'm going to say a sentence that answers a lot of questions. One of the questions is **why.**
• Listen: Yesterday, the baby cried because she had a rash.
• Listen again: Yesterday, the baby cried because she had a rash.
• Your turn. Say the sentence. Get ready. (Signal.) *Yesterday, the baby cried because she had a rash.*

2. That sentence has words that tell **why.** Everybody, **why** did the baby cry? (Signal.) *Because she had a rash.*

3. Listen: Yesterday, the baby cried because she had a rash.
   - Who cried? (Signal.) *The baby.*
   - **When** did the baby cry? (Signal.) *Yesterday.*
   - **What** did the baby do? (Signal.) *Cried.*
   - **Why** did the baby cry? (Signal.) *Because she had a rash.*

4. (Repeat step 3 until firm.)

5. Everybody, say the whole sentence. Get ready. (Signal.) *Yesterday, the baby cried because she had a rash.*
   - Which words tell who cried? (Signal.) *The baby.*
   - Which word tells **when?** (Signal.) *Yesterday.*
   - Which words tell **why?** (Signal.) *Because she had a rash.*

6. (Repeat step 5 until firm.)

Teaching Notes

The children may make mistakes in step 3 when you ask What did the baby do? Some children may say, *Cried because she had a rash.*

To Correct

1. Tell the children The answer is cried.
2. Then ask Why did she cry?
3. Then ask What did she do?
This new order makes it easier for the children to identify the part that tells why and the part that tells what she did.

How questions are the final type presented in Grade 1 Language Arts. They are introduced in lesson 36:
Here's the introduction.

EXERCISE 2

WHO–HOW–WHY

1. Some sentences have words that tell **how** somebody did things.

2. Listen: She ate slowly. **How** did she eat? (Signal.) *Slowly.*
   - Listen: She ate without looking up. **How** did she eat? (Signal.) Without looking up.

3. Listen: The boys slept soundly because they had done a lot of work.
   - Say the sentence. Get ready. (Signal.) *The boys slept soundly because they had done a lot of work.*
   - How did the boys sleep? (Signal.) *Soundly.*
   - Listen again: The boys slept soundly because they had done a lot of work.
   - **Who** slept soundly? (Signal.) *The boys.*
   - **How** did they sleep? (Signal.) *Soundly.*
   - **Why** did they sleep soundly? (Signal.) *Because they had done a lot of work.*

4. (Repeat step 3 until firm.)

5. Everybody, say the whole sentence. Get ready. (Signal.) *The boys slept soundly because they had done a lot of work.*
   - Which words tell **who?** (Signal.) *The boys.*
   - Which two words tell **what** they did? (Signal.) *Slept soundly.*
   - Which word tells **how** they slept? (Signal.) *Soundly.*
   - Which words tell **why?** (Signal.) *Because they had done a lot of work.*

6. (Repeat step 5 until firm.)

Teaching Notes

Some parts that tell **how** have only one word (quickly, well, etc.). Other parts that tell **how** have more than one word. In step 3 you present a sentence that answers questions about **who, how,** and **why.**

If children have trouble, tell them the answer to any question they miss, then repeat step 3. For the remainder of the program children review parts of sentences that answer **who, what, when, where,** and **why.** This work makes it easier for children to learn grammar. The questions that answer **who** are nouns or pronouns. The questions that answer **what** are verbs. The questions that answer **what, where,** and **why** are part of the sentence's predicate.

QUESTIONING SKILLS

The questioning-skills track begins in lesson 18 on the worksheet and lesson 25 as an oral activity and continues through the end of the program. The track is designed to show children how to seek information through questions. The track presents efficient ways for them to do this. In the first exercises you tell them that you're thinking of an object. Children ask specific questions that you answer. Then children identify the object.

Here's the oral exercise from lesson 25:

EXERCISE 1

QUESTIONING SKILLS

1. I'm thinking of an object. You'll ask questions to figure out what that object is. You'll ask these questions:
- What class is it in?
- What parts does it have?
- Where do you find it?
2. Listen to the questions again.
- What class is it in?
- What parts does it have?
- Where do you find it?
3. Everybody, say all three questions.
- Question 1. (Signal.) *What class is it in?*

- Question 2. (Signal.) *What parts does it have?*
- Question 3. (Signal.) *Where do you find it?*
4. Ask question 1. Get ready. (Signal.) *What class is it in?*
- It's in the class of furniture.
5. Ask question 2. Get ready. (Signal.) *What parts does it have?*
- It has a top and drawers.
6. Ask question 3. Get ready. (Signal.) *Where do you find it?*
- You find it in the bedroom.
7. Raise your hand when you know the object. ✔
- Everybody, what object was I thinking of? (Signal.) *A dresser.*
8. (Repeat steps 4 through 7 until firm.)

The final exercise type of questioning skills starts in lesson 86. The exercise embeds question-asking in a story context. You start telling a story that contains words that not all children will know. The children tell you to stop when they hear such a word, and then they ask a question about the meaning of the word.

EXERCISE 6

QUESTIONING SKILLS

1. I'm going to tell a story. When you hear a word you don't know, say **stop.**
2. A boy was looking at an (pause) **illustration.** (Children should say *stop.*)
- Everybody, what word don't you know? (Signal.) *Illustration.*
- Ask the question about what the word illustration means. Get ready. (Signal.) *What does the word illustration mean?*
- I'll tell you what illustration means. Illustration is a synonym for **picture.** What is illustration a synonym for? (Signal.) *Picture.*
- If the boy was looking at an illustration, he was looking at a . . . (Signal.) *picture.*
3. Here's more of the story.

- The picture showed a large (pause) **feline.** (Children should say *stop*.)
- Everybody, what word don't you know? (Signal.) *Feline.*
- Ask the question about what the word feline means. Get ready. (Signal.) *What does the word feline mean?*
- I'll tell you what feline means. Feline is a synonym for cat. What is feline a synonym for? (Signal.) *Cat.*
- So if the boy was looking at an illustration of a feline, he was looking at a picture of a . . . (Signal.) *cat.*
4. Here's more of the story.
- The boy said: "That is a cat I (pause) cherish." (Children should say *stop*.)
- Everybody, what word don't you know? (Signal.) *Cherish.*
- Ask the question about what the word cherish means. Get ready. (Signal.) *What does the word cherish mean?*
- I'll tell you what cherish means. Cherish means adore. What does cherish mean? (Signal.) *Adore.*
- So if the boy cherished the cat, he adored the cat.
5. So then the boy took the illustration of the feline he cherished and hung it on his wall. That's the end of the story.

Teaching Notes

- The pacing of this format should be quite rapid. Treat this task as a game.

- Remember to pause before saying each "new" word.

- If the children's responses are firm in steps 1 and 2, you can simply tell them, Ask the question, after they tell you to Stop.

- Praise them for good performance.

OTHER ACTIVITIES

The sentence skills track demonstrates how to ask questions about function, location, parts, class, and color. It also teaches children how to ask about the meaning of a word.

Here are suggestions for additional activities:

Start by showing the children a paper bag. Tell the group they have just ten questions to find out what's in the bag. Remind them of the strategies they've learned, such as asking about the class it's in, how it's used, where you find it, and what are its parts.

When you're explaining things outside the Language lessons remind the children, If you hear a word you don't understand, say Stop.

Finally, reinforce questions that children ask each other or you. If children ask a good question (one that will yield important information), praise them. That's a really good question.

VERB TENSE

The verb tense track begins in lesson 43 with a review of the concepts **yesterday, today,** and **tomorrow.** After these are firm, children are taught to use the appropriate tense for each time. For example: Yesterday the man sat on his porch. Today the man sits on his porch. Tomorrow the man will sit on his porch. The pairing of time notation (yesterday, today, tomorrow) with words that indicate the tense (sat, sits, will sit) provides the children with framework for understanding some of the tense conventions.

The verb tense track presents both regular and progressive forms (sat, was sitting) in both singular and plural statements.

Here's the exercise from lesson 43.

EXERCISE 5

VERB TENSE

1. Listen. Tomorrow the cars **will be** on the street. Today the cars **are** on the street. Yesterday the cars **were** on the street.
2. I'll make the statement about the cars tomorrow. Tomorrow the cars will be on the street.
   - Your turn. Make the statement about the cars tomorrow. Get ready. (Signal.) *Tomorrow the cars will be on the street.*
3. I'll make the statement about the cars today. Today the cars are on the street.
   - Your turn. Make the statement about the cars today. Get ready. (Signal.) *Today the cars are on the street.*
4. I'll make the statement about the cars yesterday. Yesterday the cars were on the street.
   - Your turn. Make the statement about the cars yesterday. Get ready. (Signal.) *Yesterday the cars were on the street.*
5. (Repeat steps 2 through 4 until firm.)
6. Listen to these statements.
   - Today the car **is** on the street.
   - Tomorrow the car **will be** on the street.
   - Yesterday the car **was** on the street.
7. Make the statement about the car today. Get ready.(Signal.) *Today the car is on the street.*
8. Make the statement about the car tomorrow. Get ready.(Signal.) *Tomorrow the car will be on the street.*
9. Make the statement about the car yesterday. Get ready.(Signal.) *Yesterday the car was on the street.*

Teaching Notes

The exercise seems simple, but some children have serious problems with tense because they practice saying things in a way that is different from formal English or school English. For instance, they may say, *Yesterday it's cold;* or *Yesterday it cold.*

Give the children enough practice in saying the statements the right way so they remember how to say them. Do not simply correct mistakes and assume that the corrections will make a difference in their performance on the next verb-tense exercise. Instead, repeat steps 7, 8, and 9 until the children's responses are very firm when saying the statements.

Through similar exercises, children review the use of the words **are** and **were.**

In lesson 98, children discriminate whether statements tell what somebody **did** or what somebody **will do.**

Here's the exercise from lesson 98:

EXERCISE 5

VERB TENSE

1. It's time for some statements.
2. Listen. The baby will cry. Say that statement. Get ready. (Signal.) *The baby will cry.*
   - Does that statement tell what the baby did or what the baby will do? (Signal.) *What the baby will do.*
3. Listen. The baby cried. Say that statement. Get ready. (Signal.) *The baby cried.*
   - Does that statement tell what the baby did or what the baby will do? (Signal.) *What the baby did.*
   Through similar exercises the children review tense and number (singular-plural) for different statement types that present problems for some children.

STATEMENTS

This track begins in lesson 59 and contiues to the end of the program. The major objectives of the track are to demonstrate what a simple satement tells about an event and what it **does not tell.** Here's the exercise from lesson 59.

EXERCISE 4

STATEMENTS

1. Listen to this statement. The girls are jumping rope.
- Everybody, say that statement. Get ready. (Signal.) *The girls are jumping rope.*
2. Does that statement tell what the girls are doing now? (Signal.) *Yes.*
- Does that statement tell what the girls did yesterday? (Signal.) *No.*
- Does that statement tell if the girls are happy? (Signal.) *No.*
- Does that statement tell if the girls are wearing shoes? (Signal.) *No.*
- Does that statement tell how many girls are jumping rope? (Signal.) *No.*

3. The girls are jumping rope. Everybody, say that statement again. Get ready. (Signal.) *The girls are jumping rope.*
4. Here's one thing that statement does not tell us. It doesn't tell how long the rope is. Your turn to name two more things the statement does not tell us. (Call on individual children. Repeat both correct responses.)
5. You named two things the statement does not tell us.
- Everybody, name the first thing. Get ready. (Hold up one finger.) (The group repeats the first response.)
- Everybody, name the second thing. Get ready. (Hold up two fingers.) (The group repeats the second response.)
6. (Repeat step 5 until firm.)

Teaching Notes

If the children have trouble with step 4, model a number of examples: The statement tells about the girls. But it doesn't tell what kind of girls. It doesn't tell whether they are young, fat, smart, whether they have long hair or short, brown eyes or blue. It doesn't tell what they are wearing.

The statement tells what the girls are doing— jumping rope. It doesn't tell where they are jumping rope. Are they in the park? On the sidewalk? Are they having a good time?

Before presenting the exercise in lesson 59, make sure that you can **name at least ten things that the statement doesn't tell.** Rehearse these responses so that you can act quickly when children have trouble naming things **not** addressed in the statement.

REASONING SKILLS

The tracks in the reasoning skills group are: **same–different, true–false, can do, only, descriptions, analogies, questions and clues,** and **if–then.** The common features of these tracks are:

1. These exercises deal with problem-solving. They involve relationships between objects and events rather than a single feature of an object or event. Here are some examples: Make up a statement that is true of only the boat. Why can't this be the man we're looking for? Tell me the clues that let you know I was thinking of a frog. I'll tell you where the person is. Then you have to describe that person. To correctly respond to these instructions, the children must understand and express relationships.

2. The instructions to the child are fairly complex. Instead of asking such questions as What color is this? or What class is this object in? the teacher says, for example: Tell me if what I say is true of only the boat or if it is true of the boat and the car, or If a table has a girl on it, what is under it? The responses called for in these tasks usually consist of complete statements.

3. All the concepts used in these exercises have been taught. They are applied to figure out the answers to problems.

SAME–DIFFERENT

The same–different exercises in Grade 1 review and extend the skills that were taught in the Kindergarten level. These tracks reinforce the fact that same may mean that something about two or more things is identical, not necessarily that everything about these objects is identical. Things are "the same" because they have the same function, are found in the same place, have the same pattern, have the same parts, or they are in the same class.
The objectives of this track are:
1. To teach that different is the opposite of same.

2. To teach children to compare objects and make observations about how those objects are the same and how they are different.
The first same–different exercise appears in lesson 8.

EXERCISE 4

SAME-DIFFERENT

1. We're going to tell how things are the same and how they are different.
- Listen: a bird and an airplane. See if you can think of some ways they are the same. (Call on individual children. Accept reasonable responses such as: They both fly.)
2. My turn. I'm going to name some ways they are different.
- Listen: A bird is an animal, but an airplane is not an animal. Everybody, say that. Get ready. (Signal.) *A bird is an animal, but an airplane is not an animal.*
- That's one way they are different.
- Listen: A bird has eyes, but an airplane does not have eyes. Everybody, say that. Get ready. (Signal.) *A bird has eyes, but an airplane does not have eyes.*
- That's another way they are different.
3. Now it's your turn.
- Name a way that a bird and an airplane are different. (Call on individual children. For appropriate responses, say:) Everybody, say that. Get ready. (Signal.)

Teaching Notes

This exercise reviews what children have learned in the Kindergarten level. You give children examples of how two objects are different, then they make observations of their own.

To Correct

If the children do not produce any responses in step 3, repeat step 2. Then present step 3 again. Praise the children even if they only repeat the responses you suggested. Then suggest another response. Keep prompting until the children originate responses.

Through the end of the level, different versions of this exercise are presented. You name two objects or events. Children name some ways they are the same and some ways they are different. You direct the group to repeat each acceptable response. This practice prepares children for later work when they are asked to compare things. The comparison involves doing what they have been practicing—naming important ways the things being compared are the same and different.

TRUE–FALSE

The **true–false** track sets the stage for the **only** and **description** tracks. Its goal is to demonstrate that a statement may report on what is observed or known (in which case the statement is **true**); the statement may contradict what is observed or known (in which case the statement is **false**); or the statement may refer to details that can't be confirmed/nor contradicted (in which case the statement **may be true** or **may be false.**)

The first exercise demonstrates statements that are "right," or about which you can say, are true. Those that are not right are false.

Here's the exercise from lesson 14:

EXERCISE 5

TRUE-FALSE

1. I'm going to make statements about a truck.
- Say **yes** if I make a statement that is right. Say **no** if I make a statement that is not right.
- What are you going to say if I make a statement that is right? (Signal.) *Yes.*
- What are you going to say if I make a statement that is not right? (Signal.) *No.*
2. Listen. A truck is good to eat. Is that right? (Signal.) *No.*
- Listen. A truck can carry things. Is that right? (Signal.) *Yes.*
- Listen. A truck is a piece of furniture. Is that right? (Signal.) *No.*
- Listen. A truck has hands. Is that right? (Signal.) *No.*
- Listen. A truck has wheels. Is that right? (Signal.) *Yes.*
3. Listen again. This time say **true** if I make a statement that is right. Say **false** if I make a statement that is not right.
- What are you going to say if I make a statement that is right? (Signal.) *True.*
- What are you going to say if I make a statement that is not right? (Signal.) *False.*
4. Listen. A truck is good to eat. Is that true or false? (Signal.) *False.*
- Listen. A truck can carry things. Is that true or false? (Signal.) *True.*
- Listen. A truck is a piece of furniture. Is that true or false? (Signal.) *False.*
- Listen. A truck has hands. Is that true or false? (Signal.) *False.*
- Listen. A truck has wheels. Is that true or false? (Signal.) *True.*
5. (Repeat step 4 until firm.)

Teaching Notes

In step 2, the children respond to a series of statements by saying either **yes** or **no.** In step 4 the same series is presented. This time the children respond with **true** or **false.**

Present the statements in step 2 rapidly but pause before asking the questions so that the children will have time to consider their answer to each question.

A different type of exercise begins in lesson 42. In this exercise the children identify and make up statements that are true and false.

Here's the exercise from lesson 42:

EXERCISE 8

TRUE-FALSE

1. I'm going to make statements about beds. You'll say true or false.
2. Listen. You put blankets on beds. Is that true or false? (Signal.) *True.*
   - Listen. You can sleep on a bed. True or false? (Signal.) *True.*
   - Listen. Beds grow in the ground. True or false? (Signal.) *False.*
   - Listen. You see a bed in a bedroom. True or false? (Signal.) *True.*
   - Listen. Beds are covered with stone. True or false? (Signal.) *False.*
   - (Repeat step 2 until firm.)
3. I'm going to say statements. Some of these statements are true and some are false. You tell me about each statement.
4. Cows lay eggs. True or false? (Signal.) *False.*
   - Water is dry. True or false? (Signal.) *False.*
   - Birds have feathers. True or false? (Signal.) *True.*
   - A bottle is a container. True or false? (Signal.) *True.*
   - Trees grow in the clouds. True or false? (Signal.) *False.*
5. My turn. I'm going to make up a statement about cows that is true. Listen. Cows sometimes live in barns. That statement is true.
6. Your turn. You make up a statement about cows that is true. (Call on one child. Praise an acceptable answer and have the group repeat it. Then say:) Everyone, that statement is . . . (Signal.) *true.*
7. Make up another statement about cows that is true. (Call on another child. Praise an acceptable answer and have the group repeat it. Then say:) Everyone, that statement is . . . (Signal.) *true.*
8. My turn. I'm going to make up statements about cows that are false. Listen. Cows say meow. Cows have feathers. Cows are plants. Those statements are false.
9. Your turn. You make up a statement about cows that is false. (Call on one child. Praise an acceptable answer and have the group repeat it. Then say:) Everyone, that statement is . . . Signal.) *false.*
10. Make up another statement about cows that is false (Call on another child. Praise an acceptable answer and have the group repeat it. Then say:) Everyone, that statement is . . . (Signal.) *false.*

Teaching Notes

The children are not to make statements containing the word **not** in steps 9 and 10. If they are allowed to do this, they will get the mistaken idea that all positive statements are true and that negative statements are false. This will lead to serious trouble later.

Children may make up a statement that is true but that contains the word not. For example, when trying to make up a false statement about cows, a child may say something like, *Cows are not birds.*

Tell the child, You said something that is true. Cows are not birds. You have to say something that is false.

If the child continues to have trouble constructing a false statement, identify some false statements. Listen to these false statements: Cows can fly. Cows give soda pop. Cows can talk. Cows read newspapers. Those statements are false. Your turn to make up a false statement. Say something that is not true about cows.

Children may make up statements that are false but that have the word not. Tell them how to rephrase these statements so they do not have the word **not.** For example, a child may say, *Cows are not animals.*

Tell the child, Your statement is false because cows are animals. But can you name something they could be if they are not animals?

If the child starts to be confused, name some possible classes. You could say A cow is a plant, or A cow is a vehicle, or A cow is something made of bricks, or A cow is an appliance.

Remember, don't permit children to make up statements that have the word **not.**

ONLY

This track starts in lesson 18 and continues through lesson 40. In the only track children practice first identifying and then making up statements that are true either of only one object in a pair or of both objects. For example, when looking at a picture of a boat and a car, they identify (and later make up) statements about only the boat, only the car, and finally the boat **and** the car.

Only is treated as the opposite of the word **and.** The concept of **only** is somewhat tricky. For example, here is a statement that is true of a ball: It is a toy. That statement is true of a ball, but it is also true of some other things—dolls, blocks, and so forth. A statement that is true of **only** a ball would be true of a ball but of no other toys.

Here's the exercise from lesson 18:

EXERCISE 5

ONLY

1. I'm going to make statements that are true. Some of the statements will be true of **only** your eyes. Some statements will be true of **only** your teeth. Some statements will be true of **both** your eyes and your teeth.

2. Listen. You chew food with them. Is that true of only your eyes, only your teeth, or both your eyes and teeth? (Signal.) *Only your teeth.*

- Listen. You see things with them. Is that true of only your eyes, only your teeth, or both your eyes and teeth? (Signal.) *Only your eyes.*
- Listen. They are part of your head. Is that true of only your eyes, only your teeth, or both your eyes and teeth? (Signal.) *Both your eyes and teeth.*
- Listen. They are very hard. Is that true of only your eyes, only your teeth, or both your eyes and teeth? (Signal.) *Only your teeth.*
- Listen. The dentist fixes them when they have a problem. Is that true of only your eyes, only your teeth, or both your eyes and teeth? (Signal.) *Only your teeth.*
- Listen. They hurt if you hit them with a hard object. Is that true of only your eyes, only your teeth, or both your eyes and teeth? (Signal.) *Both your eyes and teeth.*

3. (Repeat step 2 until firm.)

Teaching Notes

You make statements. Some are true of only teeth; some are true of only eyes; others are true of both teeth and eyes.

Children have worked on true–false since lesson 14, so they should be firm in their understanding that true means that the statement is right and false means that it is not right.

If children make mistakes in step 2, correct the mistakes and then repeat step 2 until the children are able to go through the step without making any mistakes.
A variation of an only exercise appears in later lessons.

Here's the exercise from lesson 38:

EXERCISE 3

ONLY

1. I'm going to say a statement.
2. Listen. It is food. Say that. Get ready. (Signal.) It is food.

- Is that statement true of milk? (Signal.) *Yes.*
- Is that statement true of only milk? (Signal.) *No.*
- Name some other things it's true of. (Call on individual children. Praise all reasonable responses.)

3. Listen. You can work with it. Say that. Get ready. (Signal.) *You can work with it.*
- Is that statement true of milk? (Signal.) *No.*

4. Listen. You can drink it. Say that. Get ready. (Signal.) *You can drink it.*
- Is that statement true of milk? (Signal.) *Yes.*
- Think about this. Is that statement true only of milk? (Signal.) *No.*
- Name some other things it's true of. (Call on individual children. Praise all reasonable responses.)

5. Listen. You can drink it and it comes from cows. Say that. Get ready.(Signal.) *You can drink it and it comes from cows.*
- Is that statement true of milk? (Signal.) *Yes.*
- Think about this. Is that statement true only of milk? (Signal.) *Yes.*
- Yes, that statement is true of only milk.

Teaching Notes

Children repeat statements that are true of milk. Then children tell whether the statement is true of only milk. If not, children name other things the statement tells about. If children make mistakes, name some things the statement is true of. If children tend to make more than one mistake in the exercise, repeat the exercise until responses are firm.

CAN DO

This track begins in lesson 41 and teaches the relationship between what is being done and what **can** and **cannot** be done. For example: A boy is sitting. He **can** stand (that is, he is capable of standing); however, he **cannot fly** like a bird.

The track also teaches the children to make observations about what objects can and cannot be used for. For example: A man can read a newspaper, but a man cannot cook soup in a newspaper. Work with "can do" clarifies what is possible and what is pretend.

The "can do" exercises require children to answer questions about what can and cannot be done with a given object. Then they make up complete statements that tell about can or cannot.

Here's the exercise from lesson 41:

EXERCISE 3

CAN DO

1. Get ready to answer some questions about a pair of scissors.
2. Can you use a pair of scissors to cut paper? (Signal.) *Yes.*
- Can you use a pair of scissors to cut string? (Signal.) *Yes.*
- Can you tear a pair of scissors into little pieces? (Signal.) *No.*
- Can you drink from a pair of scissors? (Signal.) *No.*
3. (Repeat step 2 until firm.)
4. Here are some more questions about what you can do with a pair of scissors.
5. Can you put a pair of scissors into a box? (Signal.) *Yes.*
- Can you cook hamburgers with a pair of scissors? (Signal.) *No.*
- Can you step on a pair of scissors? (Signal.) *Yes.*
- Can you hide inside a pair of scissors? (Signal.) *No.*
6. (Repeat step 5 until firm.)
7. I'm going to ask you about what a woman can do with a pair of scissors.
8. Can a woman cut paper with a pair of scissors? (Signal.) *Yes.*
   Say the whole thing about what a woman can do. Get ready. (Signal.) *A woman can cut paper with a pair of scissors.*

- Can a woman write a letter with a pair of scissors? (Signal.) *No.*
  Say the whole thing. Get ready. (Signal.) *A woman cannot write a letter with a pair of scissors.*
9. (Repeat step 8 until firm.)

Teaching Notes

In steps 2 and 5 children answer yes-no questions about what someone can do with a pair of scissors. In step 8, they say complete sentences. If children make mistakes in any of these steps, repeat the step. If children make mistakes in more than one of these steps, repeat steps 2 through the end of the exercise.

In another variation, children make up statements about what someone can and cannot do with an object.

Here's the exercise from lesson 68:

EXERCISE 2

CAN DO

1. I'm going to ask questions about a woman and a paper bag.
2. Everybody, can a woman play music on a paper bag? (Signal.) *No.*
- Say the statement. Get ready. (Signal.) *A woman cannot play music on a bag.*
3. Everybody, can a woman tear a paper bag? (Signal.) *Yes.*
- Say the statement. Get ready. (Signal.) *A woman can tear a paper bag.*
4. (Call on one child.) Your turn. Make up another statement that tells something a woman can do with a paper bag. (After the child makes the statement, call on the group.)
- Say the statement about what a woman can do with a paper bag. Get ready. (Signal.) *(The group repeats the child's statement.)*
- (Repeat until firm.)
5. (Call on another child.)

Your turn. Now make up a statement that tells something a woman cannot do with a paper bag. (After the child makes the statement, call on the group.)
- Say the statement about what a woman cannot do with a paper bag. (Signal.) *(The group repeats the child's statement.)*
- (Repeat until firm.)
6. (Repeat steps 4 and 5 until firm.)

Teaching Notes

Steps 4 and 5 are the critical steps. All statements that children compose should begin with the words A woman . . . and should tell about something the woman can or cannot do with a paper bag.

Make sure that children repeat each acceptable statement. If children are weak on either step 4 or 5 call on individual children to make up statements that the group repeats. Children sometimes treat the word can as if it refers to what is allowed, not what is possible. For example: **Can** you tear a paper bag into little bits and scatter them all over the rug? Yes, you can. **Should** you do this? No. The confusion of **can** with **should** sometimes becomes apparent in step 5. Children sometimes name things they should not do with a paper bag, for example: You can't hit your brother with a paper bag.

To correct the confusion of can not and should not:
- Tell the children, You're telling me about what you **should** do.
- Firm their responses on a series of paired **should-can** statements, such as:

Should you write on the walls with crayons?
Can you write on the walls with crayons?
Should you spill your juice?
Can you spill your juice?
- Repeat step 5. When necessary, remind the children, Don't tell me what you should or should not do with a paper bag. Tell me what you can or can not do.

DESCRIPTION

The description track starts in lesson 47. The exercises in this track provide children with facts that function as clues for figuring out what object you are referring to. The first clue that you present does not identify a particular object. Rather, the first clue refers to a lot of possible objects. The next clue narrows the possibilities. The final clue limits the possibilities to one. The content that is presented in the description track dovetails with information that children have learned about only and about can do.

Here's the exercise from lesson 47:

EXERCISE 4

DESCRIPTION

1. I'm thinking of an object. See if you can figure out what object I'm thinking of. I'll tell you something about the object.
2. Listen. It's made of metal. Everybody, what do you know about the object? (Signal.) *It's made of metal.*
3. Is a can made of metal? (Signal.) *Yes.* So could I be thinking of a can? (Signal.) *Yes.*
4. Is a fish made of metal? (Signal.) *No.* So could I be thinking of a fish? (Signal.) *No.*
5. Is a baseball made of metal? (Signal.) *No.* So could I be thinking of a baseball? (Signal.) *No.*
6. Is a spoon made of metal? (Signal.) *Yes.* So could I be thinking of a spoon? (Signal.) *Yes.*
7. Listen. The object I'm thinking of is (hold up one finger) made of metal **and** (hold up two fingers) it's round.
8. Everybody, what is the first thing you know about the object? (Hold up one finger.) *It's made of metal and* (hold up two fingers) *it's round.*
9. (Repeat step 8 until firm.)
10. Is a rubber ball made of metal and is it round? (Signal.) *No.* So could I be thinking of a rubber ball? (Signal.) *No.*

- Why not? (Signal.) *It's not made of metal.*
11. (Repeat step 10 until firm.)
12. Is a coin made of metal and is it round? (Signal.) *Yes.* So could I be thinking of a coin? (Signal.) *Yes.*
13. (Repeat step 12 until firm.)
14. Is a can made of metal and is it round? (Signal.) *Yes.* So could I be thinking of a can? (Signal.) *Yes.*
15. (Repeat step 14 until firm.)
16. Listen. The object I'm thinking of is (hold up one finger) made of metal **and** (hold up two fingers) it's round **and** (hold up three fingers) you can use it to buy things in a store.
17. Everybody, name the object I am thinking of. (Pause two seconds.) Get ready. (Signal.) *A coin.* Yes, a coin.
18. How do you know I'm thinking of a coin? (Hold up one finger.) *It's made of metal and* (hold up two fingers) *it's round and* (hold up three fingers) *you can use it to buy things in a store.*
19. (Repeat step 18 until firm.)

Teaching Notes

In steps 1 and 2, you tell the children that the object you are thinking of is made of metal. You then name different objects (steps 3 through 6) and have the children test each one—is it made of metal? In step 7 you tell the children that the object is round, and in step 16 you tell them that you use it to buy things in the store.

• Each step should be presented quickly.

• Pay particular attention to step 10. The answer to Why not? is very specific. *It's not made of metal.*

• Follow the instructions for holding up fingers. The task of remembering the information is easier for the children if it is associated with finger cues.

Starting in lesson 58, children play detective. They listen to descriptions that provide clues about the identity of an object.

Here's the exercise from lesson 58:

EXERCISE 2

DESCRIPTION

1. Get ready to play detective and find out what object I'm thinking of. I'll give you two clues.
2. (Hold up one finger.) It's a building. (Hold up two fingers.) It has a lot of seats.
3. Say the two things we know about the object. Get ready.
   (Hold up one finger.) *It's a building.*
   (Hold up two fingers.) *It has a lot of seats.*
4. (Repeat step 3 until firm.)
5. Those clues don't tell you enough to find the right building. They could tell you about a lot of buildings. See how many buildings you can name that have a lot of seats.
   (Call on individual children. The group is to name at least three buildings that have a lot of seats, such as a school, a theater, and a temple.)
6. Here's another clue for finding the right object. Listen. Children go there to learn. Everybody, say that. Get ready. (Signal.) *Children go there to learn.*
7. Now here are the three things we know about the object.
   (Hold up one finger.) It's a building.
   (Hold up two fingers.) It has a lot of seats.
   (Hold up three fingers.) Children go there to learn.
8. Everybody, say all the things we know.
   (Hold up one finger.) *It's a building.*
   (Hold up two fingers.) *It has a lot of seats.*
   (Hold up three fingers.) *Children go there to learn.*
9. Everybody, tell me what I'm thinking of. (Pause) Get ready. (Signal.) *A school.*
   Yes, a school.

Teaching Notes

You provide two clues about the object in step 2. In step 3, children repeat the clues as you signal.

The clues could describe various buildings. In step 5, children identify buildings that have a lot of seats. If children have trouble lead them by asking about different buildings. Does a church have lots of seats? Does a barn have lots of seats? Does a theater have lots of seats? . . . Then repeat step 5.

You give the children another clue in step 6 and review the clues in step 7. In step 8 the children review the clues and in step 9 they identify the building.

Children may be able to identify the building before you present step 8. Do not skip step 8. Make sure that children's responses are firm when saying the three clues before you direct them to name the object you've been describing.

In lesson 67, a new kind of description exercise presents a nonsense word. This type is particularly important for children because it shows them the difference between words and meaning. Often children have trouble separating names from meanings. The type of exercise that begins in lesson 67 helps children by showing them that information about an object's characteristics doesn't come from the name of the object but from information about the object. (A rose by any other name . . .)

Here's the exercise from lesson 67:

EXERCISE 2

DESCRIPTION

Note: The children are not to memorize the "funny" name in this task.

1. I'm going to tell you about an object you know. But I'm going to call it a funny name. See if you can figure out what object I'm thinking about.

2. (Hold up one finger.)
   A tunk is a tool. Say that. (Signal.) *A tunk is a tool.*
   • (Hold up two fingers.)
   A tunk is used to pound nails. Say that. (Signal.) *A tunk is used to pound nails.*
3. Everybody, say the things you know about a tunk. Get ready.
   • (Hold up one finger.) *A tunk is a tool.*
   • (Hold up two fingers.) *A tunk is used to pound nails.*
4. (Repeat steps 2 and 3 until firm.)
5. Everybody, tell me the kind of tool I am calling a tunk. (Pause.) Get ready. (Signal.) *A hammer.*
6. I couldn't fool you. It's really a hammer. How do you know a tunk is a hammer? (Call on a child. Idea: *It's a tool. It's used to pound nails.*)
7. How would you like to eat with a tunk? *(Children respond.)*

Teaching Notes

Treat this exercise as a game. Smile, and act as if you enjoy presenting it.

Note how you first signal with one finger, then two, in steps 2 and 3.

Don't allow the children to identify the object at the end of step 2. Tell them, Don't say the answer yet. Then repeat step 2.

Don't leave step 3 until the children are saying both statements correctly.

If the children give the wrong answer in step 5, correct as follows:

1. Say the things you know about a tunk.
2. Ask What tool do you use to pound nails?

The work with descriptions provides children with the mind set that words are simply tools that tell about objects and events. If a new word describes the same thing that familiar words describe, the words mean the same thing. They are synonyms. The work with synonyms begins in lesson 77, after children have worked extensively with description exercises.

ANALOGIES

Worksheet analogies begin in lesson 49. The oral work on the analogies track begins in lesson 65. The track is designed to give children practice in applying what has been taught about classification and sameness. It provides children with practice in expressing different analogous relationships. Analogy skills are important because they form one of the basic reasoning strategies for generalizing to new experiences or they organize new facts. The children learn to:

1. Complete analogies. (Red is to stop as green is to . . .)
2. Construct analogies that follow a specific rule. (Make up an analogy that tells how a bird and a fish move. A bird is to flying as a fish is to swimming.)
3. Tell what analogies are about. (A baseball is to throwing as a banana is to eating. What does that analogy tell about the objects? What you do with them.)

The first exercises in the track introduce children to the statements that are used in analogies. Instead of saying *A bird is like an airplane,* children say, *A bird is an airplane.*

Here's the exercise from lesson 65:

EXERCISE 6

ANALOGIES

1. You're going to make up sentences that are like the sentence I start with.
2. Listen: Your shoe is for some part of your body. What part? (Signal.) *Your foot.*
   Yes, your shoe is for your foot.
   • Everybody, say that. Get ready. (Signal.) *Your shoe is for your foot.*
3. Your glove is for . . . (Signal.) *your hand.*
   • Say the statement about your glove. Get ready. (Signal.) *Your glove is for your hand.*
4. Your shoe is for . . . (Signal.) *your foot.*
   • Say the statement about your shoe. Get ready. (Signal.) *Your shoe is for your foot.*

5. Your hat is for . . . (Signal.) *Your head.*

• Say the statement about your hat. Get ready. (Signal.) *Your hat is for your head.*

6. Your belt is for . . . (Signal.) *Your waist.*

• Say the statement about your belt. Get ready. (Signal.) *Your belt is for your waist.*

In this exercise, children are presented with statements of the form, Your shoe is for your foot.

The work that children will do later in the program assumes that their responses are firm when making these statements. If you are in doubt, give the children individual turns.

In lesson 68, children do tasks similar to those from lesson 65 except that they also say the statement a different way.

Here's the exercise from lesson 68.

EXERCISE 5

ANALOGIES

1. You're going to make up sentences that are like the sentence I start with.

2. Listen: A magazine is made of some material. What material? (Signal.) *Paper.* Yes, a magazine is made of paper.

• Everybody, say the statement. Get ready. (Signal.) *A magazine is made of paper.*

3. What material is a window made of? (Signal.) *Glass.*

• Say the statement about a window. Get ready. (Signal.) *A window is made of glass.*

4. What material is a towel made of? (Signal.) *Cloth.*

• Say the statement about a towel. Get ready.(Signal.) *A towel is made of cloth.*

5. What material is a coin made of? (Signal.) *Metal.*

• Say the statement about a coin. Get ready. (Signal.) *A coin is made of metal.*

6. What material is a board made of? (Signal.) *Wood.*

• Say the statement about a board. Get ready. (Signal.) *A board is made of wood.*

7. We'll talk about the same things, but we'll use a different type of statement.

8. Listen: A window is to glass. Say the statement. Get ready. (Signal.) *A window is to glass.*

9. Listen: A coin is to metal. Say the statement. Get ready. (Signal.) *A coin is to metal.*

10. Listen: A towel is to cloth. Say the statement. Get ready. (Signal.) *A towel is to cloth.*

11. Listen: A magazine is to paper. Say the statement. Get ready. (Signal.) *A magazine is to paper.*

Teaching Notes

Through step 6 children make statements that tell what the objects are made of. In step 7 you tell the children that you're talking about the same things, but you're using a different type of statement. Starting with step 8, they use the statement form **window is to glass.** The exercise does not call for individual turns, but if you're in doubt about whether children are saying the statements properly, present individual turns.

After children have practiced saying the statements that are used in analogies for several lessons, children make up their first analogy.

Here's the exercise from lesson 69:

EXERCISE 6

ANALOGIES

1. We're going to make up an **analogy.** What are we going to make up? (Signal.) *An analogy.*

• An analogy tells the way things are the same and the way they're different.

2. We're going to make up an **analogy** that tells how animals move.

• What is the analogy going to tell? (Signal.) *How animals move?*

3. Here are the animals we're going to use in the analogy: A bird and a fish.
   Which animals? (Signal.) *A bird and a fish.*

4. Name the first animal. Get ready. (Signal.) *A bird.*

• Yes, a bird. Tell me how that animal moves. Get ready. (Signal.) *It flies.*

5. Here's the first part of the analogy. Listen. A bird is to flying. Say the first part of the analogy. Get ready. (Signal.) *A bird is to flying.*
   Yes, a bird is to flying.

6. The second animal is a fish.

• Tell me how that animal moves. Get ready. (Signal.) *It swims.*

7. Here's the second part of the analogy. Listen. A fish is to swimming. Say the second part of the analogy. Get ready. (Signal.) *A fish is to swimming.*
   Yes, a fish is to swimming.

8. (Repeat steps 3 through 7 until firm.)

9. My turn. I'm going to say the whole analogy. First I'm going to tell how a bird moves, and then I'm going to tell how a fish moves. Listen. A bird is to flying as a fish is to swimming.

10. Let's say the analogy together. Get ready. *A bird is to flying **as** a fish is to swimming.*

11. All by yourselves. Say the analogy that tells how a bird moves and how a fish moves. Get ready.(Signal.) *A bird is to flying as a fish is to swimming.*

12. (Repeat step 11 until firm.)

Teaching Notes

In step 1, you introduce the word analogy, and in step 2 you tell the children about the analogy they are going to make up.
After you lead the children through the analogy, you say the whole analogy in step 9. Make sure you have good rhythm when you present the analogy, and be sure to stress the word as. You may want to say the word as so it clearly divides between the parts of the analogy.

A bird is to flying (Pause) **as** (Pause) a fish is to swimming.
Make sure you say the analogy the same way when you say it with the children.
In step 11, the children say the analogy by themselves. Make sure they say all the words clearly. If you're in doubt present individual turns, then repeat step 11. If children learn to say the analogy correctly, they will find the following analogy exercises much easier than they would if their responses were not firm with the wording.
In lesson 75, children make up two analogies that involve the same categories. The categories are a deer and a fish. Children first make up an analogy to tell how the animals move. Next they make up an analogy that tells where you find the animals.

Here's the exercise from lesson 75:

EXERCISE 1

ANALOGIES

1. We're going to make up **two** analogies.

• We're going to make up analogies about a deer and a fish. Which animals? (Signal.) *A deer and a fish.*

2. The first analogy tells how the animals move.

• How does a deer move? (Call on a child. Accept all reasonable answers, but use: *Runs.*)

• How does a fish move? (Signal.) *Swims.*

3. So a deer is to running as a fish is to . . . (Signal.) *swimming.*

• Say that analogy about a deer and a fish. Get ready.(Signal.) *A deer is to running as a fish is to swimming.*

4. Listen: A deer is to running as a fish is to swimming. Does the analogy tell **where** you **find** the animals? (Signal.) *No.*

5. Listen: A deer is to running as a fish is to swimming. Does that analogy tell how the animals move?(Signal.) *Yes.*

6. Listen: A deer is to running as a fish is to swimming. Does that analogy tell what parts the animals have? (Signal.) *No.*
7. (Repeat steps 4 through 7 until firm.)
8. We made up an analogy that tells how the animals move. The next analogy tells where you find the animals.
   - Where do you find a deer? (Call on a child. Accept all reasonable answers, but use: *in the forest.*)
   - Where do you find a fish? (Call on a child. Accept all reasonable answers, but use: *in the water.*)
9. A deer is to the forest as a fish is to the . . . (Signal.) *water.*
   - Say that analogy about a deer and a fish. Get ready. (Signal.) *A deer is to the forest as a fish is to the water.*
10. We made up an analogy that tells how the animals move. Then we made up an analogy that tells where you find the animals. Let's see if you can say both those analogies.
11. Think. Say the analogy that tells how the animals move. (Pause.) Get ready. (Signal.) *A deer is to running as a fish is to swimming.*
    - Think. Say the analogy that tells where you find the animals. (Pause.) Get ready. (Signal.) *A deer is to the forest as a fish is to the water.*
12. (Repeat step 11 until firm.)

Teaching Notes

Make sure that children's responses are firm in the steps through 9. In step 11 children say both the analogies. If children make mistakes on step 11 repeat the step but not always with the tasks in the same order. For example, tell them: Say the analogy that tells how they move . . . Say the analogy that tells how they move . . . Say the analogy that tells where you find the animals . . . Say the analogy that tells how they move.

Try to make sure that the children's responses are firm for the pair of analogies before leaving the lesson.

Children work on similar analogy pairs through lesson 81. In lesson 82 children use what they have learned about analogies to identify what an analogy is about.

Here's the exercise from lesson 82:

EXERCISE 1

ANALOGIES

1. You're going to figure out what an analogy is about.
2. Listen to this: A boat is to water as an airplane is to . . . (Signal.) *air.*
3. What class are a boat and an airplane in? (Signal.) *Vehicles.*
   - Yes, vehicles. Our analogy tells something about vehicles.
4. A boat is to water as an airplane is to air.
   - Does our analogy tell where you find the vehicles? (Signal.) *Yes.*
   - Does our analogy tell what parts they have? (Signal.) *No.*
   - Does our analogy tell what they are made of? (Signal.) *No.*
   - Does our analogy tell what color they are? (Signal.) *No.*
   - Our analogy tells where you find them.
   - (Repeat step 4 until firm.)
5. Where do you find a boat? (Signal.) *In water.*
   - Say the **first** part of the analogy. Get ready. (Signal.) *A boat is to water.*
6. Where do you find an airplane? (Signal.) *In air.*
   - Say the **next** part of the analogy. Get ready. (Signal.) *An airplane is to air.*
7. Tell me what the analogy tells about the vehicles. Get ready. (Signal.) *Where you find them.*
8. Everybody, say the whole analogy. Get ready. (Signal.) *A boat is to water as an airplane is to air.*
9. (Repeat steps 7 and 8 until firm.)

Teaching Notes

Make sure that children are correct when identifying what the analogy is about in step 4. Also make sure that responses are firm in steps 7 and 8. If children make mistakes on exercises of this type, firm them. Then repeat the same exercise at the beginning of the next language lesson.

Later exercises in the track are like the exercise in lesson 82 except that you present more than one analogy that refers to the same objects. For instance, in lesson 110 children analyze two analogies that involve in paint brush and a hammer.

• A paint brush is to painting as a hammer is to . . .

• A paint brush is to bristles as a hammer is to . . .

Children complete the analogies and indicate what each tells about the tools.

The work with analogies reinforces what children have learned about descriptions and classification. The work provides children with a useful mental framework for telling how things are the same.

QUESTIONS AND CLUES

Questions and Clues are used as a kind of classification game that relates to binary-logic activities. The general format for Questions and Clues involves starting with a set of objects and using information from a "clue" to eliminate some objects. The procedure is repeated until all but one object is eliminated and children have discovered the mystery object.

After children have learned the general format of using clues, they generate questions for finding the "mystery picture." The objective for many activities is to find the mystery picture by asking only three questions. These activities shape children's strategy for generating "smart" questions, those that will systematically eliminate possibilities.

The first "clue" activity is introduced in lesson 82. Here's part of the introduction:

Name _____

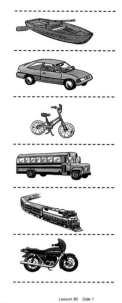

Lesson 85 Side 1

5. You're going to play a mystery game. It's a very hard game. Here's how it works: I'll tell you clues about the mystery vehicle. After each clue, you'll be able to fold over some pictures that could **not** be the mystery vehicle. After I give you the last clue, you'll know which vehicle is the mystery vehicle because it will be the **only** picture that is **not** folded over. Does that game sound pretty tough?

6. Here's the first clue about the mystery vehicle: This vehicle has wheels. Everybody, say that clue. (Signal.) *This vehicle has wheels.*

• Not all the vehicles have wheels. If it does **not** have wheels, it can **not** be the mystery vehicle. So fold over any vehicle that does **not** have wheels. Just turn it over the way you would turn a page in a book. Raise your hand when you're finished.
(Observe children and give feedback.)

• Everybody, which vehicle did you fold over? (Signal.) *The rowboat.*

• Why did you fold over the rowboat? (Call on a child. Idea: *A rowboat does not have wheels.*)

7. Here's another clue about the mystery vehicle: This vehicle has windows. Everybody, say that clue. (Signal.) *This vehicle has windows.*

- Listen: If it does **not** have windows, it can **not** be the mystery vehicle, so fold over any vehicle that does not have windows. Raise your hand when you're finished. (Observe children and give feedback.)

- Which vehicles did you fold over? (Call on a child. Idea: The bicycle and motorcycle.)

- Why did you fold over the bicycle and motorcycle? (Call on a child. Idea: *A bicycle and a motorcycle do not have windows.*)

8. Here's another clue about the mystery vehicle: This vehicle can hold **more** than ten people. Everybody, say that clue. (Signal.) *This vehicle can hold more than ten people.*

- Listen: If it can **not** hold more than ten people, it can **not** be the mystery vehicle, so fold over any vehicle that can **not** hold more than ten people. Raise your hand when you're finished. (Observe children and give feedback.)

- Everybody, which vehicle did you fold over? (Signal.) *The car.*

- Why did you fold over the car? (Call on a child. Idea: *A car cannot hold more than ten people.*)

9. Here's the last clue about the mystery vehicle: This vehicle runs on tracks. Everybody, say that clue. (Signal.) *This vehicle runs on tracks.*

- Listen: Fold over the picture that could **not** be the mystery vehicle. ✔

- Everybody, which vehicle did you fold over? (Signal.) *The bus.*

- Why did you fold over the bus? (Call on a child. Idea: *A bus does not run on tracks.*)

10. You figured out which vehicle is the mystery vehicle. It should be the **only** picture that is **not** folded over. Everybody, which vehicle is the mystery vehicle? (Signal.) *The train.*

- Raise your hand if you figured out the mystery vehicle. ✔

11. I gave you four clues that let you figure out the mystery vehicle. Let's see how many of those clues you remember.

- What was one of the clues? (Call on a child. Accept appropriate response.)

12. What was another clue? (Call on a child. Accept appropriate response.) (Repeat step 12 until all clues have been identified.)

13. Who can name all four clues about the mystery vehicle? (Call on several children. Praise any child who can name at least three clues.)

14. You did such a good job on the mystery game that we'll play it again next time.

In the steps not shown here, children identify the objects and the class, and they cut "flaps" (cut along the dotted lines).

Teaching Notes

Children often have trouble folding the flaps so they stay in place. Direct them to pull the flap to the right as far as it goes and then press down with a ruler very hard. Children sometimes have trouble with the notion that if a picture cannot be the mystery vehicle, they should then fold it over. Present the wording in steps 6 through 9 very carefully. If children have trouble, repeat this part of the exercise. Children will use variations of this procedure on many later lessons. It's important, however, for them to have a good idea of why they folded over each object.

There are also exercises that require children to generate questions about the mystery picture. In these activities, you prompt the kind of questions they should ask. Beginning in lesson 97, you divide the class into 4 teams. Children work cooperatively. Each team develops three questions that will lead to the identification of the mystery object.

Children first cut the flaps. Here's the part of the exercise that follows.

3. Now, let's play the toughest game of all. We'll see which teams can do it. Remember, if you're **really** smart, your team can find the mystery picture by asking only **three** questions. But they have to be **super** questions. You're working in teams. So your team has to agree on each question before the team asks it. Everybody on a team figures out which questions your team will ask. When your team has your first question, raise your hands and I'll come over. You'll whisper the question to me so that none of the other teams can hear the question. I'll whisper the answer, and you'll fold over the pictures that could **not** be the mystery picture.

4. (Key: The target picture is 7—one dog sitting next to a doghouse.)

- You know your **first** question is good if you can fold over **four** pictures after I answer your first question. Remember, you're trying to find the mystery picture in only **three** questions. Raise your hands when your team has a good question.

  Answers:
  (How many dogs?) One.
  (What is the dog doing?) Sitting.
  (Where is the dog?) Next to a doghouse.
  (Do **not** combine answers, such as: **Sitting next to** a doghouse.)

5. (After you answer each team's question, tell the team to fold over the pictures that could not be the mystery picture. Then ask them if that was a good question. Remind them by saying:) For a good first question, you can fold over four pictures.

- (Then direct each team to agree on the next question. Tell them:) If it's a good question, you can fold over two pictures.

- (Repeat the procedure for the third question:) If it's a good question, you'll know which picture is the mystery picture.

6. (After any team has found the mystery picture by asking only three questions, tell the class:) We have a winner. We have a team that found the mystery picture by asking only three questions.

- (Call on a team member to say the three questions. Do not accept "combined" questions.)

7. Everybody, what's the number of the mystery picture? (Signal.) *Seven.*

- How many dogs are in that picture? (Signal.) *One.*

- What is the dog doing? (Signal.) *Sitting.*

- Where is the dog? (Signal.) *Next to a doghouse.*

Teaching Notes

Do not accept combined questions (2 questions), such as, "Are there two dogs and are they standing?" Questions like, "Are two dogs standing next to the doghouse?" are not acceptable. They are often not good questions. (If the answer is "yes," you know the picture. If the answer is "no," you have learned very little.)

When you answer questions, make sure that you do not give additional information. If children ask, "Where are the dogs?" for their first question, don't reject the question or indicate that there's only one dog. Just say, "I'll tell you where. Next to the doghouse." Do not say, "Sitting next to the doghouse."

Similarly, if children ask, "What are the dogs doing?" just say, "Sitting." Don't say, "Sitting next to the doghouse."

In earlier lessons, children learned the rule that, if their first question is good, they should be able to turn over half the pictures (in this case, four pictures). Use this rule when giving feedback on the first question. "If you can't turn over four pictures, that was not a very good question."

When children work cooperatively, praise teams that have their three questions formulated quickly. Let the other teams know that this behavior is desirable. "Team C already has its questions. That's really working together well."

Also praise groups for working quietly. "I can't hear the things that team B is saying. They're working hard, but none of the other groups can hear them."

IF–THEN

On lesson 94 children are introduced to two-picture sequences that show an action and the result of the action. For instance, in lesson 100, Clarabelle is walking out on a diving board in the first picture. In the second the diving board is breaking. Children follow along the arrow and say the two parts of the if-then statement: If Clarabelle walks out on the diving board, the diving board will break.

On lesson 109 children work with a chain of two if-thens. Children first say the if-then statement for the first arrow: *If Clarabelle sits on a chair, the chair will break.* Then they say the if-then statement for arrow 2. This if-then starts with the second picture: *If the chair breaks, Clarabelle will fall on the floor.*

After children work with the two if-then statements, you direct them to say both rules.

8. Everybody, get ready to say both rules. Say the rule for arrow 1. (Signal.) *If Clarabelle sits on a chair, the chair will break.*

• Say the rule for arrow 2. (Signal.) *If the chair breaks, Clarabelle will fall on the floor.*
   (Repeat step 8 until firm.)

Teaching Notes

Make sure children are firm on step 8. If some children are still making mistakes after you present step 8 two or three times, make a note of their problem, reassure them that this is a tough task and present it again at a later time (preferably before lesson 35).

The problem the children will most likely have is stating the second if-then. Remind them: "Remember, for arrow 2, you start with **if** and tell about the second picture; then tell about the third picture."

Starting with lesson 116, the children practice expressing causal statements that start with **if**; for example, *If you drop raw eggs, they will break.*

Here's the exercise from lesson 119:

EXERCISE 6

IF–THEN

1. You're going to make up if–then statements.
2. Listen: Which ice would melt, ice that is in a freezer or ice that is on a table? (Signal.) *Ice that is on a table.*
3. Start with the words "If ice is," and say the whole statement. Get ready. (Signal.) *If ice is on the table, it will melt.*
4. (Repeat steps 2 and 3 until firm.)

5. Listen: Which door will not open, a door that is locked or a door that is unlocked? (Signal.) *A door that is locked.*
6. Start with the words, "If a door is locked," and say the whole statement. Get ready. (Signal.) *If a door is locked, it will not open.*
7. (Repeat steps 5 and 6 until firm.)
8. Let's do those statements again.
9. Say the statement that tells about ice that is on the table. Get ready. (Signal.) *If ice is on the table, it will melt.*
10. Say the statement that tells about a door that is locked. Get ready. (Signal.) *If a door is locked, it will not open.*
11. (Repeat steps 9 and 10 until firm.)

Teaching Notes

This part of the if–then track is fairly short, but you should make sure that the children learn how to say if–then statements. Often children understand the logic of if–then, but they may phrase the statements quite differently. *You do that and you get in trouble.* (If you do that, you'll get in trouble.)

If you don't feel that the program provides children with enough practice with if–then statements, have the children construct additional examples. Here's an example: If you're hungry, what do you want to do? Say the whole statement . . . If you're thirsty, what do you want to do? . . . Say the whole statement. If you're tired, what do you want to do? . . . Say the whole statement.

DIRECTIONAL SKILLS

Many teaching demonstrations and worksheet instructions used in the primary grades assume that children understand the meaning of such terms as **from** and **left**. Children are also expected to be able to read and understand simple maps.

The exercises in the directional skills track are designed to teach these basic concepts. The specific objectives are:

1. To teach the meaning of the words **from, to, north, south, east,** and **west.**
2. To provide adequate practice in making statements that contain these words.

FROM–TO

The introduction of from–to is provided through a worksheet exercise in lesson 32. Here's the student material and the exercise:

WORKSHEET 32 EXERCISE 8

FROM–TO

1. Everybody, find the next page in your workbook. ✔
   (Hold up workbook.) Find the black dog. ✔
2. The **black dog** is moving **from** the circle to the triangle. What is the dog moving **from?** (Signal.) *The circle.*
   • What is the dog moving **to?** (Signal.) *The triangle.*
3. (Repeat step 2 until firm.)
4. Touch the thing the dog is moving **from.** ✔
   Everybody, what are you touching? (Signal.) *The circle.*

• Touch the thing the dog is moving **to.** ✔
   Everybody, what are you touching? (Signal.) *The triangle.*
5. Here's the rule about the thing the dog is moving **to.** It should be yellow. Name the thing you are going to color yellow. Get ready. (Signal.) *The triangle.*
   • Make a yellow mark on the thing the dog is moving to.
   (Observe children and give feedback.)
   • Here's a rule about the thing the dog is moving **from.** It should be blue. Name the thing you are going to color blue. Get ready. (Signal.) *The circle.*
   • Make a blue mark on the thing the dog is moving **from.**
   (Observe children and give feedback.)
6. Touch the **spotted dog.** ✔
   • That dog is moving from something to something else. Touch the thing the dog is moving **from.** ✔
   • Everybody, what is the dog moving **from?** (Signal.) *The circle.*
   • Touch the thing the dog is moving **to.** ✔
   • Everybody, what is the dog moving **to?** (Signal.) *The triangle.*
7. The rule is the same for **all** the dogs. The thing the dog is moving **to** should be yellow. Name the thing you are going to color yellow. (Signal.) *The triangle.*
   • Make a yellow mark on the thing the spotted dog is moving **to.**
   (Observe children and give feedback.)
   The thing the dog is moving **from** should be blue. Name the thing you are going to color blue. (Signal.) *The circle.*
   • Make a blue mark on the thing the spotted dog is moving **from.**
   (Observe children and give feedback.)
8. Now make marks for a **white dog.** Make a yellow mark on the thing that dog is moving **to.** ✔
   • Make a blue mark on the thing that the dog is moving **from.** ✔
9. Later you'll fix the other white dog.

Teaching Notes

By introducing from–to in worksheet activities, you provide children with the concrete information they need to appreciate how from–to actually works.

In step 2, you tell the children what the black dog is doing—moving from the circle to the triangle. You ask what the dog is moving from and to.

In step 4, children touch the thing the dog is moving from. Make sure they are touching the circle. If they are not, repeat steps 2 and 3.

Use the same strategy for mistakes in step 4. Starting with step 6, the children identify what the spotted dog is moving from and what it is moving to. You do not first model the responses the children are to make. They are to figure out the responses from looking at the picture. Children should not have serious problems with this exercise.

Through lesson 36, children work with similar coloring rules that involve from–to. In lesson 37, you present actual instances of something moving from one place to another. These exercises require children to observe the movement and figure out where the movement went from and where it went to.

Here's the exercise from lesson 37:

EXERCISE 2

FROM–TO

1. (Draw a small circle on the chalkboard.)
- Get ready to tell me if I move my finger from the circle.
2. (Place your finger to the left of the circle.) Watch. (Move it toward the circle.)
- Did I move from the circle? (Signal.) *No.*
3. (Place your finger inside the circle. Move it straight up from the circle.)
- Did I move from the circle? (Signal.) *Yes.*
4. (Place your finger inside the circle.) Watch. (Move it from the circle to the left.)
- Did I move from the circle? (Signal.) *Yes.*
5. (Place your finger above the circle.) Watch. (Move it straight down to the circle.)

- Did I move from the circle? (Signal.) *No.*
6. (Place your finger inside the circle.) Watch. (Move it from the circle to the right.)
- Did I move from the circle? (Signal.) *Yes.*
7. (Place your finger below the circle.) Watch. (Move it straight up to the circle.)
- Did I move from the circle? (Signal.) *No.*
8. (Repeat steps 2 through 7 until firm.)
9. (Place your finger inside the circle.) Watch. (Move it below the circle.)
- Did I move from the circle? (Signal.) *Yes.*
- How did I move my finger? (Signal.) *From the circle.*
- Say the whole thing about how I moved my finger. Get ready. (Signal.) *You moved your finger from the circle.*
10. (Repeat step 9 until firm.)

Teaching Notes

For this exercise, you draw a circle on the chalkboard. You move your finger from the circle or toward the circle. After each move, you ask the children, Did I move **from** the circle?

If children make mistakes repeat steps 1 through 7 until responses are firm.

The development of from–to continues largely throughout worksheet activities that are similar to the one presented in lesson 32. These activities provide the children with practice in linking their knowledge of from–to with rules for coloring different objects.

MAP READING

The map reading exercises begin in lesson 46. They teach the children the names of the four directions—**north, south, east,** and **west.** They also teach decoding simple maps, facing different directions, and moving in different directions. These exercises also make sure of the previously taught concepts from and to.

The introduction of the four directions requires you to make small signs and place them on the appropriate walls of the room. You then show the children that the name on the wall you face tells the direction you are facing.

Here's the exercise from lesson 46:

EXERCISE 7

MAP–READING

Note: Make sure **north, south, east,** and **west** cards are placed on the appropriate walls.

1. Everybody, we're going to learn about directions. What are we going to learn about? (Signal.) *Directions.*

2. (Point north.) The signs on the walls show the four directions. (Point to each sign and read them in this order:) North, south, east, west.

3. Your turn. I'll point in different directions. You tell me the directions.
   - (Point north.) Everybody, which direction is this? (Signal.) *North.*
   - (Point south.) Everybody, which direction is this? (Signal.) *South.*
   - (Point east.) Everybody, which direction is this? (Signal.) *East.*
   - (Point west.) Everybody, which direction is this? (Signal.) *West.*

4. (Repeat step 3 until firm.)

5. (Move to the middle of the room.) Look at me. I'm going to walk. You point to the wall I'm walking to. That's the direction I'm walking.

6. Watch. (Walk toward the south wall.) Everybody, which direction? (Signal.) *South.*
   Yes, I walked south.
   - (Return to the middle of the room.)

> **Error:**
>
> The children don't say *south.*
>
> **Correction:**
>
> 1. (Point to the south wall.) Which wall am I pointing to? (Signal.) *The south wall.*
> 2. So which direction am I pointing? (Signal.) *South.*
> 3. (Repeat step 6.)

7. Watch. (Walk toward the north wall.) Everybody, which direction? (Signal.) *North.*
   Yes, I walked north.
   - (Return to the middle of the room.)

8. (Repeat steps 6 and 7 until firm.)

> **Teaching Notes**
>
> - Arrange the signs before the Language period so that you don't lose time with the children.
> - Place the signs so that you will be walking in the appropriate direction when you move from your starting position to the signs. You should actually walk south to reach the south sign.
> - In step 5, make sure that children are pointing to the sign on the south wall.
> - If children make mistakes or produce weak responses in the later steps of the exercise, direct them to point to the wall you are walking to.
>
> In the following lessons, you present variations of the basic exercise. You walk in different directions. Children name the directions. The signs continue to be on the wall and children refer to the signs when figuring out the directions.
>
> In lesson 50, you introduce a variation that requires children to face different directions and make statements about the directions they face. The signs should still be on the appropriate walls.

Here's the exercise from lesson 50:

EXERCISE 8

MAP–READING

1. Let's all stand up. (Signal.) *(All stand.)*

2. I'm going to face east. Watch. (Face the east wall.)
   - What am I doing? (Signal.) *Facing east.*
   - Say the statement. (Signal.) *You are facing east.*

3. Everybody, now you're going to face east. (Pause.) Get ready. (Signal.) *(The children face east.)*

- What are you doing? (Signal.) *Facing east.*
- Say the statement. (Signal.) *I am facing east.*

4. Everybody, you're going to face north. (Pause.) Get ready. (Signal.) *(The children face north.)*
   - What are you doing? (Signal.) *Facing north.*
   - Say the statement. (Signal.) *I am facing north.*
5. Everybody, you're going to face south. (Pause.) Get ready. (Signal.) *(The children face south.)*
   - What are you doing? (Signal.) *Facing south.*
   - Say the statement. (Signal.) *I am facing south.*
6. (Repeat steps 2 through 5 until firm.)
7. Let's sit. (Signal.) *(All sit.)*
8. (Point east.) Tell me the direction I'm pointing. Get ready. (Signal.) *East.*
   - Say the statement. Get ready. (Signal.) *You are pointing east.*
   - Yes, if I walked all day in this direction, I would be going east.
9. (Point north.) Tell me the direction I'm pointing. Get ready. (Signal.) *North.*
   - Say the statement. Get ready. (Signal.) *You are pointing north.*
   - Yes, if I walked for an hour in this direction, I would be going north.
10. (Repeat steps 8 and 9 until firm.)

Teaching Notes

Make sure that children face the correct directions. They should not simply face the sign unless they face the correct direction when they face the sign.

Do not hurry the children. Pause for several seconds before saying Get ready, particularly if children do not respond on signals. If children do have problems, repeat the exercise. Make sure that children are not copying the responses of others. If children are slow at responding, present individual turns.

Starting on lesson 52, children learn the conventions for how directions are indicated on the map.

Here's the exercise from lesson 52:

EXERCISE 6

MAP–READING

1. (Draw a large rectangle on the board. Label as indicated:)

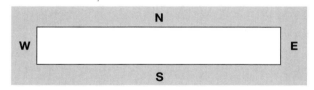

2. We're going to learn a rule about reading maps.
3. Here's the rule about maps. (Touch each letter as you say:) **North** is on the top; **south** is on the bottom; **east** is on this side; **west** is on this side.
4. (Repeat step 3.)

5. See if you can say the rule with me. Get ready. (Touch each letter as you and the children say the rule.) **North** is on the top; **south** is on the bottom; **east** is on this side; **west** is on this side.

6. Listen. **North** is on the top; **south** is on the bottom. Say that. (Touch each letter as the children respond. Do not respond with the children.) **North** is on the top; **south** is on the bottom.

7. (Repeat step 6 until firm.)

8. Listen. **East** is on this side; **west** is on this side. Say that. (Touch each letter as the children respond without you.) **East** is on this side; **west** is on this side.

9. (Repeat step 8 until firm.)

10. Now say the whole rule. (Touch each letter as the children respond. Do not respond with the children.) **North** is on the top; **south** is on the bottom; **east** is on this side; **west** is on this side.

11. (Repeat steps 6 through 10 until firm.)

12. I'm going to move my finger. Tell me the direction I go.

13. (Touch the middle of the rectangle.) Watch. (Move toward the north.) Everybody, which direction did I go? (Touch.) *North.* Yes, north. I went north.

14. (Touch the middle of the rectangle.) Watch. (Move toward the south.) Everybody, which direction did I go? (Touch.) *South.* Yes, south. I went south.

15. (Touch the middle of the rectangle.) Watch. (Move toward the west.) Everybody, which direction did I go? (Touch.) *West.* Yes, west. I went west.

16. (Repeat steps 12 through 15 until firm.)

17. Let's say the rule about the map one more time. (Touch each letter as you and the children say the rule.) **North** is on the top; **south** is on the bottom; **east** is on this side; **west** is on this side.

Teaching Notes

You start by drawing a large rectangle on the board and lettering the sides to show the four directions.

Practice saying the rule about the map in step 3 rhythmically and expressively. Some children will require a lot of repetition before they can say the rule. The practice will be far more pleasant if what they are trying to say sounds like a lively poem.

When practicing the rule, touch each side of the map as you say the appropriate direction.

- If children are unable to say the entire rule of step 6 after six or more trials, let them know that they are doing a good job, acknowledge that the rule is very hard, and tell them that you will return to the rule later. Before the end of the lesson, try to get in a few more practice trials.

- If the children have trouble saying the rule, follow the model, lead, and test procedure. Say the part of the rule they are having trouble with. Have them say that part with you, then test them on that part. Then add another part and repeat the model, lead, and test procedure.

- Some students may have trouble with steps 12 through 17 particularly if the map is not drawn on the north wall. (If it is drawn on the south wall, for example, a movement to the right is moving east on the map, but toward the west wall of the room.)

- Point out the difference between the map and the room. You're telling me about the directions in **this room.** But that's not the rule for the map. You have to look at the side of the map I'm moving to.

- Give a few examples. Start at the middle of the map and move your finger north. Ask, Which side of the map did I move to? Then ask, So which direction did I go? Repeat with south, then do east and west.

- When children respond correctly to the examples, repeat steps 12 through 17 until responses are firm.

The basic exercise above is repeated on the next lesson. At the end of that lesson, children's responses should be firm on the rule for maps. In lesson 54, children do their first worksheet exercise involving maps (north on the top, south on the bottom). The early exercises show arrows facing different directions. Children identify arrows that face north, for example, and make them a particular color.

The development of the map skills provides children with a solid foundation for understanding how to interpret maps and how to make them.

INFORMATION

The two main information tracks present calendar information and information about materials (concrete, plastic, wood, etc.). Additional information is provided through worksheet activities where children learn about the features of particular locations (such as the doctor's office or a forest) and about the parts of common objects.

DAYS, MONTHS, AND SEASONS

This track starts in lesson 2 and continues throughout the level. It teaches the children the following information:
1. The names of the days of the week, the months, and the seasons.
2. The number of days in a week, a month, and seasons in a year; the number of days and weeks in a year.
3. The meaning of yesterday, today, and tomorrow.
4. How to locate and interpret dates on a calendar.

This track begins with exercises that review what the children were taught in the kindergarten level. Here's a review exercise from lesson 2:

EXERCISE 3

CALENDAR FACTS

1. Here are facts about days and dates.

- Listen: There are seven days in a week. Say the fact. Get ready. (Signal.) *There are seven days in a week.*
- When you name the days of the week you start with Sunday. Listen: Sunday, Monday, Tuesday, Wednesday, Thursday, Friday, Saturday.
- Your turn. Start with Sunday and say the seven days of the week. Get ready. (Signal.) *Sunday, Monday, Tuesday, Wednesday, Thursday, Friday, Saturday.*
2. New fact: There are four seasons in a year.
- Everybody, say the fact. Get ready. (Signal.) *There are four seasons in a year.*
3. (Repeat step 2 until firm.)
4. When you name the seasons, you start with the first season of the year. That's winter. Listen: winter, spring, summer, fall.
- Your turn. Name the four seasons of the year. Get ready. (Signal.) *Winter, spring, summer, fall.*

Teaching Notes

The children who have gone through the Kindergarten level should know this material. A goal of the program is to make sure that the children learn this information thoroughly enough for it to become automatic. If children's responses are firm, go through the exercise quickly.

Also in lesson 2, children are introduced to the calendar. Here's the exercise:

EXERCISE 6

CALENDAR

Note: You will need a current calendar for steps 3 through 6.
1. Everybody, how many days are in a week? (Signal.) *Seven.*
- Start with Sunday and say the days. Get ready. (Signal.) *Sunday, Monday, Tuesday, Wednesday, Thursday, Friday, Saturday.*
2. (Repeat step 1 until firm.)
3. (Present calendar. Point to the month.) Listen: This month is _____.

What's this month? (Signal.)

- This is a calendar. It shows the dates. Those are the numbers of the days for this month.
- The calendar shows days of the week. The first column shows Sunday. (Point to Sunday column.) The next column shows Monday. (Point to Monday column.) The next column shows Tuesday. (Point to Tuesday column.)

4. I'll touch columns. You tell me if I'm touching numbers for Sunday, Monday, or Tuesday.

- (Touch a number for Sunday.) What day? (Signal.) *Sunday.*
- (Touch another number for Sunday.) What day? (Signal.) *Sunday.*
- (Touch a number for Monday.) What day? (Signal.) *Monday.*
- (Touch another number for Monday.) What day? (Signal.) *Monday.*
- (Touch a number for Sunday.) What day? (Signal.) *Sunday.*
- (Touch a number for Monday.) What day? (Signal.) *Monday.*
- (Touch a number for Tuesday.) What day? (Signal.) *Tuesday.*
- (Touch a number for Monday.) What day? (Signal.) *Monday.*
- (Touch a number for Tuesday.) What day? (Signal.) *Tuesday.*
- (Touch another number for Tuesday.) What day? (Signal.) *Tuesday.*

5. I'll show you the number for today. (Touch number. Say date: day, month, number; e.g.: Today is Wednesday, September 15th.)

- Your turn. Say the date.(Signal.)

6. (Repeat step 5 until firm.)

Teaching Notes

You will need a calendar, ideally a large one that shows the entire month. A reproducible blank calendar appears at the end of this guide. This calendar provides cells for up to 6 weeks.

This exercise acquaints children with the conventions of the calendar. Each column shows a particular day. All the dates shown in the column are the same day, shown during different weeks.

In the steps that precede 4, you show children how the columns work. Practice this routine before presenting to the children so that you don't have to keep referring to the script. Remember, you're going to show children that everything in the first column is a Sunday and everything in the next column is a Monday. You'll go back and forth from column to column so that children will learn to distinguish between the columns.

In step 5, you show children the number for the current date. When you tell them the date, remember to say, for example, Today is Thursday, September 14th. (You may add the year if you wish; however, the information that is relevant to the calendar is the day of the week and the number for the day.)

On later lessons, children learn new calendar information. It is integrated with the information they have already learned and reviewed regularly.

From lesson 30 until the end of the program, children are asked to say the date that is one week from today. Fill in the first part of the upcoming month when this information is called for in the lesson.

MATERIALS

The list below shows the materials that are taught or reviewed in Grade 1 and shows the lesson in which the material first appears.

Materials	Lessons
Plastic	16
Cloth	16
Paper	16
Wood	18
Graphite	18
Rubber	18
Leather	20
Glass	30
Concrete	36
Metal	36

The materials track starts in lesson 16 and continues through lesson 114. Children review the materials information they learned in the Kindergarten level; throughout the level, they learn new information about materials.

Here's part of the review from lesson 16:

EXERCISE 5

MATERIALS

1. (Present the three circles.)
   We're going to learn what things are made of.
   - (Point to the circles.) Everybody, what are these? (Signal.) *Circles.*
   Yes, circles.
2. (Point to the paper circle.)
   This circle is made of paper. What is it made of? (Signal.) *Paper.*
   - (Point to the cloth circle.)
   This circle is made of cloth. What is it made of? (Signal.) *Cloth.*
   - (Point to the plastic circle.)
   This circle is made of plastic. What is it made of? (Signal.) *Plastic.*

3. I'll point to each circle. You tell me what it is made of.
4. (Point to the plastic circle.) What is this circle made of? (Signal.) *Plastic.*
   - (Point to the cloth circle.) What is this circle made of? (Signal.) *Cloth.*
   - (Point to the paper circle.) What is this circle made of? (Signal.) *Paper.*
5. (Repeat step 4 until firm.)

Teaching Notes

For this exercise, you will need circles made of plastic, cloth, and paper. Children should be familiar with these materials; however, in the introductory exercise you name the materials before asking children to identify them.

The critical step of the exercise is step 4. Make sure that children's responses are firm in step 5 before you leave the exercise. In some of the later exercises, children integrate information that have learned about part–whole and materials.

Here's the exercise from lesson 24:

EXERCISE 1

MATERIALS

Note: You will need a wooden pencil with an eraser and a point.

1. (Touch the eraser.)
   - Everybody, what is the name of this part? (Signal.) *The eraser.*
   - (Touch the point.)
   - Everybody, what is the name of this part? (Signal.) *The point.*
   - (Touch the shaft.)
   - Everybody, what is the name of this part? (Signal.) *The shaft.*
2. (Repeat step 1 until firm.)

3. (Touch the eraser.)
 • What is the name of this part? (Signal.)
   The eraser.
 • What is this part made of? (Signal.)
   Rubber.
 • (Touch the point.)
 • What is the name of this part? (Signal.)
   The point.
 • What is this part made of? (Signal.)
   Graphite.
 • (Touch the shaft.)
 • What is the name of this part? (Signal.)
   The shaft.
 • What is this part made of? (Signal.) *Wood.*
4. (Repeat step 3 until firm.)
5. (Ask individual children the following
   questions. Accept reasonable responses.)
 • Why do you think the eraser is made of
   rubber?
 • Why do you think the shaft is made of
   wood?
 • Why do you think the point is made of
   graphite?

Teaching Notes

You present a wooden pencil with a visible
eraser and point. Children identify the parts of
the pencil (which information has been taught
in the kindergarten level and has been
reviewed throughout worksheet exercises)
and then identify the material that each part is
made of. Children who are placed
appropriately in the program should have no
trouble with this type of application.

A common review exercise directs children to
name objects that are made of different
materials.

Here's the exercise from lesson 36:

EXERCISE 5

MATERIALS

1. Think of things that are made of leather.
2. Let's see who can name at least three
   things made of leather. (Call on individual
   children to name objects made of leather.
   Each child should name at least three
   things.)
3. Think of things that are made of metal.
4. Let's see who can name at least three
   things made of metal. (Call on individual
   children to name objects made of metal.
   Each child should name at least three
   things.)
5. Think of things that are made of concrete.
6. Let's see who can name at least three
   things made of concrete. (Call on
   individual children to name objects made
   of concrete. Each child should name at
   least three things.)

Teaching Notes

In step 2 children name things that are made of leather. If children do not readily name things that are made of leather, name some things that are made of leather. You could also ask questions, such as, Do you ever wear something made of leather around your waist? What do you wear? Do you ever wear anything made of leather on your feet? What do you wear? Did you ever sit on anything made of leather? What did you sit on?

Sometimes, children give suspicious responses. For instance, they may say that pants are made of leather. The best way to clarify whether the children are knowledgeable about leather pants is to say something like this:
Is anyone in this room wearing pants made of leather?
When would a person wear pants that are made of leather?

The exercise that requires children to name things that are made of a specified material recur throughout the program. It is important for children to be facile with this type of information. From time to time, call on a child and direct her to name four or five things that are made of a particular material.

APPLICATIONS

Two tracks apply rules to different situations. They are absurdities and temporal sequencing. In the absurdities track, children are presented with situations that have a serious incongruity or inconsistency. Children identify what is absurd and tell why it is absurd. In the temporal sequencing track, children identify a sequence of events or perform a sequence of events according to verbal directions.

ABSURDITIES

This track begins in lesson 9. The early exercises are similar to those that children had worked with in the Kindergarten level. The exercise in lesson 9 reviews the meaning of absurdity and presents examples of it. Here's the exercise:

EXERCISE 7

ABSURDITY

1. Listen: Things that are very silly are **absurd.**
   What's another word for very silly? (Signal.) *Absurd.*
2. Why do we need hats? (Call on a child. Praise good answers such as: *to protect our heads; to keep our heads warm.*)
3. Why do we need shoes? (Call on a child. Praise good answers such as: *to protect our feet; to keep our feet warm.*)
4. Would you wear a hat on your arm? (Signal.) *No.*
   That would be absurd.
- Would you wear a hat on your head? (Signal.) *Yes.*
- Would you use a hat to hammer a nail? (Signal.) *No.*
   That would be absurd.
5. Remember, things that are very silly are **absurd.**

Teaching Notes

Children should not have any trouble with this exercise. They tend to like the absurdity track. If you respond to the absurdities as if they are funny, children will tend to respond in the same way.

If children are new to the program, however, they may not receive enough practice with the word absurd. For these children you could present the following task at the beginning of the next few lessons:
You learned another word for very silly. What word is that?

The absurdity track presents different types of absurdity, and these relate to the different tracks in the program, parts that are absurd, actions that are absurd, materials that are absurd, absurd sequences of events, objects that are in an absurd location, and objects that are put to absurd uses.

TEMPORAL SEQUENCING

This track begins in lesson 14 and continues through lesson 29. Its goal is to sharpen the children's understanding of how to sequence events. This skill is very important for reading comprehension and retelling. The work with temporal sequencing also provides children with skills that they use in worksheet applications of temporal sequencing.

Here's the exercise from lesson 14:

EXERCISE 3

SEQUENCE

1. I'll tell you four things that happened. Listen.
- First, the man put on ice skates.
- Next, the man went out on the ice.
- Next, the man skated.
- Last, the ice cracked.
2. Listen again.
- First, the man put on ice skates.
- Next, the man went out on the ice.
- Next, the man skated.
- Last, the ice cracked.
3. Tell me the four things that happened.
- What happened first? (Signal.) *The man put on ice skates.*
- What happened next? (Signal.) *The man went out on the ice.*
- What happened next? (Signal.) *The man skated.*
- What happened last? (Signal.) *The ice cracked.*
- (Repeat step 3 until firm.)
4. I'll say the four things, but I'm going to make mistakes. As soon as you hear a mistake, say **stop,** then tell me the right thing that happened.
- Listen. First the man put on skates. Next, the man skated. (Children say stop.)
- What happened just after the man put on ice skates? (Signal.) *He went out on the ice.*
5. Listen again. First, the man put on ice skates. Next, the man went out on the ice. Next, the ice cracked. (Children say *stop*.)

- What happened just after the man went out on the ice? (Signal.) *The man skated.*
6. Everybody, say all four things in the right order. Get ready. (Signal.) *First, the man put on skates. Next, the man went out on the ice. Next, the man skated. Last, the ice cracked.*

Teaching Notes

If the children have trouble remembering all the events in step 3, repeat step 2 but hold up a finger for each event. If children continue to make mistakes, correct it and point out the number. Listen: The man skated. That's the third thing that happened. Remember, three fingers for the man skated.

After children respond correctly in step 3, repeat step 3 without using the finger prompt. The main thing you should tell children who don't remember the events is that everything that is done is in a sensible order. The ice won't crack unless something makes it crack. So the man must skate before the ice cracks.

In step 4, the children should respond immediately to your mistakes. If children take more than a second to respond, they are not sufficiently firm on the sequence. Repeat step 3.

LANGUAGE WORKSHEETS

Most lessons have one workbook page that relates to the Language Concepts Strand. A second page relates to either the story Grammar Strand or the Writing Stand. Some of the worksheet activities are fairly structured; others are more independent.

The worksheets extend what the children are being taught during the other parts of the lessons. In some cases, the worksheets provide the primary teaching. This situation occurs when the skill or concept being taught must be illustrated, as it is with some sequencing and map reading skills.

Below is a list of the primary categories that appear on the worksheets. The lesson of the first appearance of each category is indicated.

Category	First Appearance
Classification	Lesson 1
Part—Whole	Lesson 1
Locations	Lesson 9
Questioning Skills	Lesson 18
From—To	Lesson 32
Materials	Lesson 38
Analogies	Lesson 49
Map Reading (writing directions)	Lesson 54
Story–Related Activities (what characters say, sequencing events, data collection)	Lesson 1
Writing Opposites	Lesson 112

The purpose of the worksheets is to strengthen what children learn. The goal is for children to produce responses that clearly indicate that they know important facts and relationships. Grade 1 *Language Arts* uses several response formats that are capable of yielding clear indications of the children's knowledge and possibly of the problems they have with specific skills or information.

One format involves coloring rules. You give the children directions to color all the examples of a certain type of color. In classification exercises, for instance, you might direct them to color all the appliances green. For part–whole, you might direct children to color the handle of the object blue. Another generic format requires children to draw lines to connect or categorize things that go together. For instance, for an analogy that tells about things and the parts they have, you direct children to draw lines from objects to their parts (from a boy to an arm and from a tree to a branch.)

A third generic format requires children to write. A classification exercise may direct children to write the name of the furniture or container under each of the illustrated objects.

Here's a brief summary of the various worksheet categories.

CLASSIFICATION

Most of the early classification exercises present coloring rules.

Here's the worksheet from lesson 14:

The coloring rules are: color the animals orange; color the food purple. Children do not do the coloring at this time. Instead they make a colored mark on one of the objects. For instance, they mark one of the animals orange. That mark indicates that they are to color all the animals orange.

Some of the later coloring rules are more complicated. They contain the words **some, or,** and **and.**

Here's the exercise from lesson 28 that presents directions that refer to **all** and **some.**

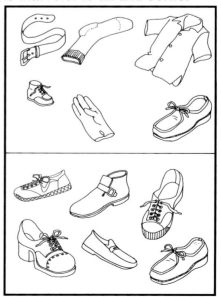

CLASSIFICATION

1. (Hold up workbook. Point to second half.) The box shows two pictures. Some of the things in one picture are shoes. All of the things in the other picture are shoes.

2. Touch the picture where some of the things are shoes. ✔

• Here's the rule about the picture where some of the things are shoes. The shoes should be green. What's the rule? (Signal.) *The shoes should be green.*

• Fix up the picture where some of the things are shoes. ✔

3. Here's the rule about the picture where all of the things are shoes. The shoes should be yellow or black. What's the rule? (Signal.) *The shoes should be yellow or black.*

• Make a yellow mark on one shoe and a black mark on another shoe. ✔

One picture shows some things that are shoes. The rule for that picture is: the shoes should be **green.**

The other picture shows only shoes. The rule for that picture is: the shoes should be **yellow** or **black.** (Children make a black mark on one shoe and a yellow mark on another shoe in this picture. The mark shows that the shoes may be either yellow or black.)

Some classification worksheets require children to write the class names for objects in the picture.

Here's the student material from lesson 89:

food	vehicles

Children write the name **food** next to each food and the name **vehicle** next to each vehicle.

Some of the later classification activities present two pictures, one showing a smaller class and the other showing a larger class.

In lesson 101, children identify the smaller class (people) and the larger class (living things) and then follow a coloring rule for the people in each picture.

Here's the student material from lesson 101:

PART–WHOLE

Children review part–whole nomenclature at the beginning of the program. Part–whole worksheet activities occur throughout the level.

Here's an early part–whole activity from lesson 4:

WORKSHEET 32 EXERCISE 8

PART–WHOLE

1. Everybody, find the next page in your workbook. (Hold up workbook.) Your page should look just like mine. ✔

2. Touch the first part of your page. (Point to the first half of the page.) You should be touching this part of your page. ✔

3. Find the picture of the pencil. Here's a coloring rule for the pencil. Listen. Color the eraser green. What's the rule? (Signal.) *Color the eraser green.*
- Mark the eraser. ✔
4. Here's another coloring rule for the pencil. Listen. Color the shaft blue. What's the rule? (Signal.) *Color the shaft blue.*
- Mark the shaft. ✔
5. Part of the pencil is missing. What part is missing? (Signal.) *The point.*
- Yes, the point. Before you color the pencil, you're going to follow the dots with your pencil to make the point.
6. Here's the coloring rule for the point. Listen. Color the point yellow. What's the rule? (Signal.) *Color the point yellow.*
- Mark the point. ✔

You review the parts of a pencil. Then children complete the picture of the pencil (identifying and drawing the missing part). Then children follow coloring rules: Color the eraser green; color the shaft blue; color the point yellow.

The color designations are sometimes not what one would commonly observe. This feature of the coloring rules is purposeful. Children must attend to the details of the rule to perform the task correctly. They can't simply rely on what they know to be true of pencils—black point, yellow shaft, red eraser.

Later part–whole activities have less structure but require children to apply various coloring rules and drawing rules.

LOCATIONS

Here's a list of the various locations and when they first appear on worksheets in Grade1 Language Arts.

Location	Lesson
doctor's office	9
farm	10
garage	11
airport	12
playground	14
dentist office	16
city	18
jungle	23
beach	25
restaurant	27
fire station	32
bus station	45
beauty parlor	49
pet store	56
hospital	58

For these activities, children identify the location shown in the picture and then follow coloring rules. Here's a location picture from lesson 10.

One coloring rule is: Color some of the farm animals black and color some of the farm animals brown.
Another rule is: Color the buildings red.

QUESTIONING SKILLS

Some primary teaching for questioning skills is presented throughout the worksheet activities. The first questioning-skills exercise appears in lesson 18. Here's the student material and the activity from lesson 18:

PART–WHOLE

QUESTIONING SKILLS

1. Everybody, find the next page in your workbook. (Hold up workbook. Point to first half.)
- Find the door. ✔
- There is something in back of this door. It's either a coat, a goat, a shoe, or pants. You have to ask two questions to find out what is in back of the door.
2. Here's the first question you're going to ask. What class is it in? Everybody, ask that question. Get ready. (Signal.) *What class is it in?*
- (Repeat step 2 until firm.)
3. Here's the next question. What parts does it have?
Everybody, ask that question. Get ready. (Signal.) *What parts does it have?*
- (Repeat step 3 until firm.)
4. Let's see if you can ask both of those questions again.
- (Hold up one finger.)
  Everybody, ask the first question. (Signal.) *What class is it in?*
- (Hold up two fingers.)
  Everybody, ask the next question. (Signal.) *What parts does it have?*
- (Repeat step 4 until firm.)
5. (Hold up one finger.)
  Everybody, ask the first question again. Get ready. (Signal.) *What class is it in?*
- Here's the answer. It's in the class of clothing.
- Could it be a coat? (Signal.) *Yes.*
- Could it be a goat? (Signal.) *No.*
- Could it be a shoe? (Signal.) *Yes.*
- Could it be pants? (Signal.) *Yes.*
6. (Hold up two fingers.)
  Everybody, now ask the question about the parts. Get ready. (Signal.) *What parts does it have?*

- Here's the answer. A front, a collar, buttons, sleeves, and pockets.
7. Think hard. It's in the class of clothing. And it has a front, a collar, buttons, sleeves, and pockets. Everybody, make a red mark on the clothing in back of the door. ✔
(Pause.)
- Everybody, what was in back of the door? (Signal.) *A coat.*

First children repeat the questions they will ask to identify the object. Then they ask the questions and you answer them.

You do not ask the children to identify the object before they follow a coloring rule and mark the correct object red (step 7).

Through similar exercises, children become facile at asking questions to secure information.

FROM–TO

For these activities, an illustration shows something moving from one thing to another thing.

Here's an example from lesson 32:

Children follow two coloring rules for each arrow.
Color the thing the dog is moving to yellow.
Color the thing the dog is moving from blue.

By following the rule, the children become firm in the idea that the dog may move in any direction.

MATERIALS

Here's the student worksheet from lesson 38:

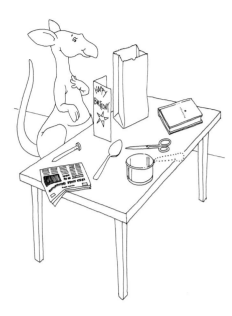

For most activities, children follow a coloring rule that directs them to color objects made of a particular material a specific color.

You present children with if–then rules: If an object is made of paper, color it green. If an object is made of metal, color it black.

Later material exercises are similar, except that some of them have more complicated rules and at least one of the objects may have a missing part. In lesson 95, for instance, children are to color things made of wood either black or brown, and things made of cloth orange. Children also draw the part that is missing from the shirt (a sleeve.)

ANALOGIES

The worksheet exercises that involve analogies parallel the oral work that children do. The first analogy worksheet exercise appears in lesson 49.

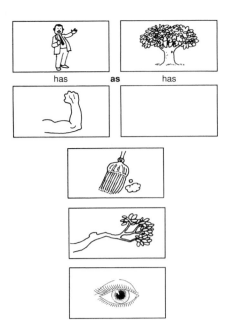

WORKSHEET 49

EXERCISE 11

ANALOGIES

1. Everybody, find the next page in your workbook. ✔
- (Hold up workbook. Point to first half.)
- The pictures show something and part of the thing.
2. Touch the man. ✔
3. Now touch the picture that's right below the man. It shows part of the man. Everybody, what part? (Signal.) *An arm.*
- Yes, those pictures show that a man has an arm.
4. Touch the tree. ✔
- One of the pictures below the tree shows the part it has. Touch the picture that shows the part a tree has. ✔
- Everybody, what part does a tree have? (Signal.) *A branch.*
5. Listen: A man has an arm as a tree has a branch.
- Tell me about a man. Get ready. (Signal.) *A man has an arm.*
- Tell me about a tree. Get ready. (Signal.) *A tree has a branch.*

6. Draw a line from the tree to the part it has. (Observe children and give feedback.)

Children show the analogous relationship between "the man has an arm" and "the tree has a branch" by drawing a line from the tree to the branch.

The worksheet activities present a full range of analogy types. Here are three different types:

Lesson 70

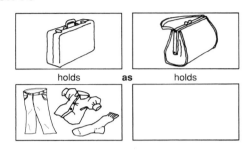

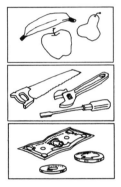

Lesson 113

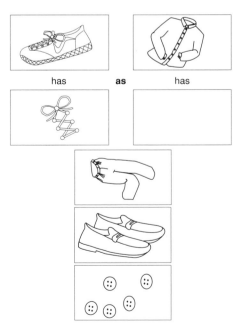

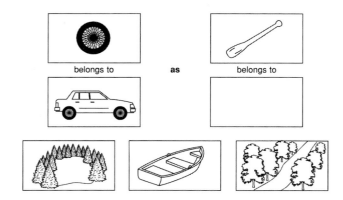

belongs to   **as**   belongs to

The analogy for the first picture is: **A suitcase holds clothes as a purse holds money.** This analogy deals with objects that accompany containers.

The analogy for the second picture is: **A shoe has laces as a shirt has buttons.** This analogy deals with the parts an object has.

The analogy for the third picture is: **A wheel belongs to a car as an oar belongs to a boat.** This analogy indicates that the object has a specified part.

MAP READING

Map reading activities begin in lesson 54. For some activities, children color arrows that show a particular direction. Here's the first exercise:

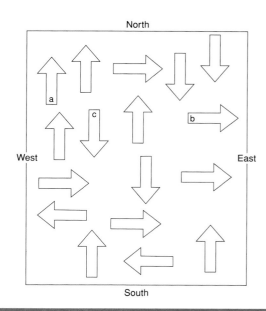

WORKSHEET 54 EXERCISE 7

MAP READING

1. Everybody, find the next page in your workbook. ✔
   (Hold up workbook. Point to first half.)
   - Some of the arrows have letters on them. Find the arrow with the letter **A.** ✔
   - That arrow is pointing **north.** Which direction? (Signal.) *North.*
2. Find the arrow with the letter **B.** ✔
   - That arrow is pointing **east.** Which direction? (Signal.) *East.*
3. Find the arrow with the letter **C.** ✔
   - That arrow is pointing **south.** Which direction? (Signal.) *South.*
4. Touch **A.** ✔
   - Everybody, which direction is that arrow pointing? (Signal.) *North.*
   - Touch **B.** ✔
   - Everybody, which direction is that arrow pointing? (Signal.) *East.*
   - Touch **C.** ✔
   - Everybody, which direction is that arrow pointing? (Signal.) *South.*
5. Listen: Here's a rule about the arrows that are pointing **north.** All arrows that are pointing **north** should be blue. What color? (Signal.) *Blue.*
   - There are six arrows that are pointing

north. Put a blue mark on each arrow that is pointing **north.**
(Observe children and give feedback.)

6. Here's a rule about the arrows that are pointing **east.** All the arrows that are pointing **east** should be red. What color? (Signal.) *Red.*

- There are five arrows pointing **east.** Put a red mark on each of them.
(Observe children and give feedback.)

7. Later you can color the arrows that are pointing **north** and the arrows that are pointing **east.**

Children have received some instructions about the directions on a map. They have just learned the directions for the four sides of the map. Children first find an arrow with a particular letter. Children then follow coloring rules such as, **All the arrows that are pointing east should be red.** For some of the later map reading, children write letters that show directions.

Here's the student material from lesson 62:

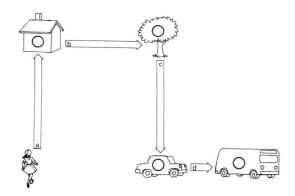

The arrows show the route the girl took to reach each object. Children write the letter of the direction the girl had to go. For instance, they write **N** in the house to show that the girl went north to reach the house.

WRITING OPPOSITES

The worksheets for opposites begin in lesson 112 and continue to the end of the level. Unlike many of the earlier tasks, the work with opposites is written.

Here's the student and teacher material from lesson 112:

rough	tall	old	pull
1. push			
2. young			
3. smooth			
4. short			

1. Everybody, find the next page. ✔
(Hold up workbook. Point to top half.) Find the words in the box at the top of your worksheet. ✔

- I'll read those words. Touch and follow along: rough, tall, old, pull. ✔

2. Your turn. Touch the first word. ✔
What word? (Signal.) *Rough.*

- Next word. ✔
What word? (Signal.) *Tall.*

- Next word. ✔
What word? (Signal.) *Old.*

- Last word. ✔
What word? (Signal.) *Pull.*

- (Repeat step 2 until firm.)

3. You're going to write words that tell the opposite.

- Touch number 1. ✔

- That word is **push.** What word? (Signal.) *Push.*

- Everybody, what's the opposite of **push?** (Signal.) *Pull.*

4. The word **pull** is in the word box. Copy that word right after the word **push.**
(Observe children and give feedback.)

5. Touch number 2. ✔

- That word is young. What word? (Signal.) *Young.*

- Everybody, what's the opposite of **young?** (Signal.) *Old.*

6. That word **old** is in the word box. Copy that word right after the word **young.**
(Observe children and give feedback.)

7. Touch number 3. ✔
- That word is **smooth.** What word? (Signal.) *Smooth.*
- Everybody, what's the opposite of **smooth?** (Signal.) *Rough.*
8. The word **rough** is in the word box. Copy that word right after the word **smooth.** (Observe children and give feedback.)
9. Touch number 4. ✔
- That word is **short.** What word? (Signal.) *Short.*
- Everybody, which word in the box is the opposite of **short?** (Signal.) *Tall.*
10. Copy the word **tall** right after the word **short.**

Children read the words. The first word is **push.** They find the word that is the opposite of push. Then they copy the word right after the word **push.** Similar exercises review the various opposites that children have learned.

STORY GRAMMAR AND LITERATURE STRAND OVERVIEW

In Grade 1 Language Arts, children learn about stories in such a way that they can construct stories according to the constraints of different story grammars.

The stories are uniquely designed for this teaching, and the sequence of stories is designed to assure that all children learn important skills associated with stories. This knowledge sets the stage for comprehension work that the children will do later in their reading program. The stories specifically address those aspects of comprehension that typically give older students trouble when reading stories.

The program teaches children how to create parallel stories based on familiar story grammars. For this teaching, model stories are introduced. Each model has a unique story grammar. Through later activities, children extrapolate the details of the model stories to create new stories with the same grammar. The activities presented in the Story-Grammar track are designed to shape children's understanding in a way that will serve them later in both reading and writing. The major presentation required to make the activities work well is to read the stories in a manner that makes them sound interesting. If you provide good reading and follow the activities, children will learn a lot about story-grammar activities. Following is a description of each of the major story characters and the story grammar that is unique to each.

PAUL

Paul has predictable behaviors:
He loves to paint—but in only two colors, pink and purple.
Paul speaks in p-starting words: "Purple plums would be perfectly pleasing."
He has a predictable solution to problems of spilled paint. If paint plops onto the porch while Paul is painting a pretty picture of purple plums, Paul says something like, "That porch looks poor with puddles of purple paint on it, but I can fix it." His solution: Paint the whole porch purple.
In the first story, purple paint gets on the pane of a window, the porch and other places. Paul solves each problem. Then his brother comes out and gets paint on his pants. His pants are a mess, but Paul says, "But brother, don't worry. I can fix it." The story doesn't tell how he does that, but the children know because the story grammar is very strong.
The children hear the model story about Paul in three different lessons. Later in the program, they use their knowledge of Paul to extrapolate. They identify unique utterances that Paul would make; they compose utterances (with p-starting words); they compose endings to new stories involving Paul and they make up entire stories.

SWEETIE

The second character introduced is a nasty cat named Sweetie, whose story grammar is completely different from Paul's. Sweetie's grammar is quite sophisticated because it always involves misunderstandings that are based on perspective.

Sweetie loves to chase things like little birds or helpless butterflies. His plans center around getting something to eat, and he says things like, "Yum, yum. I'll just go over there and grab a pawful of little brown birds."

Sweetie is always foiled because he lacks information about what really takes place when he tries to execute his plan. Sweetie always thinks that he was foiled by his helpless prey and says something like, "From here those birds look pretty helpless, but let me tell you, they are big and strong."

In the first Sweetie story, Bonnie puts up a large birdbath in the yard next door. Sweetie sees all the little birds that are attracted to the birdbath and says, "Yum, yum. Look at all those little birds. I'm going to sneak over to that birdbath. . ." So he sneaks through a hole in the fence and moves slowly through the bushes until the birdbath is within leaping range. Just then, Sweetie hears a terrible squabble in the birdbath, but he can't see what's happening. An eagle decided to take a bath, and when that eagle swooped down, all the other birds took off. Sweetie, still thinking that the little birds are in the birdbath, leaps up to grab a pawful of birds, but that eagle grabs Sweetie and slams him into the birdbath. Splash! Sweetie darts across the yard and through the hole in the fence. Finally, he peeks back at the birdbath, but in the meantime the eagle has finished its bath and taken off. The other birds have returned. Sweetie looks at them and says to himself, "From here, those birds look pretty small and helpless. But when you get close to them, they are really big and strong. I don't think I'll go near that birdbath again."

Again, the grammar is generalizable to other situations, which are presented after children have heard the model story three times. Children predict how the new stories will end, what Sweetie will say, what he thinks happened versus what actually happened. They also can identify unique utterances that Sweetie (versus Paul) might make: "Yum, yum, those are tasty looking butterflies. . ."

As with the Paul stories, the children demonstrate their knowledge of the grammar not by merely identifying characters or problems, but by creating outcomes that are consistent with the story grammar.

THE BRAGGING RATS

The next main story is about two rats who constantly argue about who is best at doing something. When describing how good they are, they go beyond exaggeration to incredible lies. After it becomes apparent to all the rats that the Bragging Rats do not know how to settle their argument, the wise old rat intervenes and shows them how to stage a contest to determine which Bragging Rat is the best. Other rats, one of whom is the little black rat, are permitted to engage in these contests. The outcome is always the same. The little black rat finishes first, and the Bragging Rats perform poorly. At the end of each story, the Bragging Rats find something else to argue about, and the other rats leave in disgust.

In the first Bragging Rats story, the rats argue about who is the fastest runner. The wise old rat sets up a course that goes to the edge of the pond and then back to the starting line. The two Bragging Rats get tangled up just before they turn around, tumble into the pond and don't finish the race. The little black rat wins. But the contest is for naught because the Bragging Rats are now arguing about who is the fastest swimmer. "I may not be the fastest runner in this bunch, but there is no rat in the world that can swim as fast as I can."

The story grammar is extrapolated to different stories and to a play about which Bragging Rat is the strongest.

CLARABELLE

Clarabelle is a cow whose story grammar is greatly different from that of Paul or Sweetie or the Bragging Rats. Clarabelle loves to imitate other animals and even people. Her plans always fail for the same reason: She's very heavy. As the first Clarabelle story says, "When she jumped into the duck pond, all the water jumped out of the pond."

The predictable aspects of the grammar are:

- Clarabelle will try to do something that

somebody else does.

- Because of her weight, she fails.
- The outcome is humorous.
- The people or animals she tries to imitate become annoyed with her.

In the first Clarabelle story, Clarabelle observes a group of bluebirds sitting on a wire attached near the hayloft of the barn. Clarabelle decides that she wants to sit on that wire with the birds. Some of the other farm animals try to warn her not to do it and remind her of some of her past fiascoes, but Clarabelle climbs up to the loft and tiptoes out onto the wire. The wire sags down under her weight, and the bluebirds are not at all happy. "This wire is for bluebirds, not brown-and-white cows."

Finally, Clarabelle decides to get off the wire. Going back into the loft would require going uphill, and Clarabelle is just above a mound of hay, so she decides to jump down from the wire. When she does, the wire springs up and shoots the bluebirds into the clouds, leaving blue feathers fluttering here and there. Naturally, the other farm animals roll around in laughter, but Clarabelle is not at all happy.

In a later parallel story, Clarabelle decides to imitate the school children who line up and get on the school bus. The bus stands up on end when she moves to the back of it.

Another Clarabelle story has Clarabelle fascinated with the idea of going off a diving board and into a swimming pool. When she does, the board breaks and everybody gets mad at Clarabelle.

ROLLA

Rolla's story grammar presents another type of "perspective" confusion. Rolla is a merry-go-round horse who wears the number 8. That number bothers her because there are only eight horses, and she's number 8. So one day she executes her plan to change her number. She thinks that if she could go faster, she could pass up the horse in front of her, and then she'd be number 7. Or better yet, she could pass up all the other horses and be number 1.

When she attempts to go faster, the other horses go faster, the music speeds up and sounds awful, and the merry-go-round goes so fast that nobody will go on it. As one mother puts it, "This is like a rodeo." Rolla becomes depressed when she realizes that her plan won't work, and the other horses are concerned because they're exhausted from streaking around in circles. They ask Rolla questions and discover her problem. They solve it by giving Rolla the number 1. Everybody is happy.

In a later story, Rolla feels that she is too close to number 8, the horse right in front of her. To create a greater distance between herself and number 8 she . . . . The children make up an ending to show how the other horses ensure that Rolla can't see horse number 8.

BLEEP

Bleep is an imperfect robot invented by Molly Mixup, whose nickname comes from the fact that none of her inventions work exactly the way they should. Although Bleep is very talented, he has some unusual personality characteristics:

He always says "bleep" at the beginning of his sentences.

He often replies to directions such as, "Get the paint from the garage," by saying, "Bleep. Okay, baby."

His verbal reports are sometimes unreliable (or confusing).

The Bleep story grammar is more complicated than those of the other characters because it is developed over a sequence of stories. The first sequence is a three-episode story in which Bleep incorrectly relays a phone message. He has a phone conversation with a friend of Molly's, Mrs. Anderson, who thinks she is talking to Molly, not Bleep. Mrs. Anderson asks if "Molly" has a preference about where the two women will meet for lunch. Bleep indicates that there is a wonderful restaurant at the corner of 13th and Elm; however, the only thing on that corner is a wrecking yard. The women arrive at different times (Molly in a red van and Mrs. Anderson in a red sports car), park their cars in front of the wrecking yard (in drop-off zones) and search for the restaurant. They run into each other and return to their respective cars, only to find that the cars have been dismantled and that the workers are ready to scrunch the remains of each vehicle. Molly gives the workers directions for reassembling the vehicles, but the results are two red vehicles—each half-sports-car and half-van. Nobody is very happy.

The Bleep story grammar is extended in later stories that involve Molly adjusting the screws in Bleep's head. Each adjustment results in unexpected changes in the way Bleep talks or in the things he remembers. In later stories, Molly must reteach Bleep the days of the week and the months of the year because he has somehow lost memory of them and replaced them with "blurp" words. So in saying the days of the week, Bleep would say, "Sunday, Monday, Tuesday, Blurpday, Blurpday . . ."

Stories

The pattern for the story exercises is for the story to be presented two or three times. With each reading of the story, a different workbook activity is presented. After the introduction of the story, children encounter new stories or activities involving familiar characters and familiar story grammars.

Here's a list of the stories and the lesson in which each story is presented.

During the introduction of a story, you ask specified questions. Later, when you reread a story, fewer questions are presented.

Here's the introduction of the story Sweetie and the Birdbath (lesson 3). The text of the story is in the ruled box.

1. Everybody, I'm going to read you a story. Listen to the things that happen in the story because you're going to have to fix up a picture that shows part of the story.
2. This is a story about a mean cat named Sweetie and the adventure he had with a birdbath. The story starts before there was a birdbath. Listen:

A woman named Bonnie loved birds. One day she noticed some birds cleaning themselves by splashing in a puddle on the sidewalk. She said, "Those birds shouldn't have to splash in a puddle to get clean. They need a birdbath." That was a good idea.

7. Listen: What did Bonnie see that gave her the idea that the birds needed a birdbath? (Call on a child. Idea: *Bonnie saw the birds splashing in a puddle.*)

The more Bonnie thought about getting a birdbath the more she liked the idea. "I will get a birdbath big enough for all the birds that want to take a bath."

So Bonnie went to the pet store and looked at birdbaths. She picked out the biggest birdbath they had.

- Listen: Where did Bonnie go to get a birdbath? (Call on a child.) *To the pet store.*
- Which birdbath did she pick out? (Call on a child. Idea: *The biggest one they had.*)

The next day, a truck delivered the birdbath. Bonnie set it up in her backyard and soon some birds saw it. They called to their friends and the first thing you know all kinds of birds were splashing in the birdbath—red birds, yellow birds, spotted birds and little brown birds.

- See if you can get a picture in your mind of that birdbath with lots of birds in it.
- What color are the birds in the birdbath? (Call on a child. Idea: Red, yellow, brown and spotted.)
- What are those birds doing? (Call on a child. Idea: *Splashing in the birdbath.*)

Following the story-reading is a workbook activity with an illustration of part of the story. Here's the picture and activities following the introduction of the Sweetie story:

EXERCISE 8

STORY DETAILS

- Everybody, open your workbook to lesson 3. Write your name on the top of the page. ✔
  Here's a picture of something that happened in the story.
7. What's Sweetie doing in this picture? (Call on a child. Idea: *Grabbing the eagle.*)
- Everybody, is Sweetie all wet yet? (Signal.) *No.*
- What's going to happen right **after** this picture is over? (Call on a child. Idea: *Sweetie will get slammed into the birdbath.*)
- Everybody, does that eagle look happy? (Signal.) *No.*
- Look in the trees.
  There are 10 birds in the trees. See if you can find all of them and color them the right colors. Who remembers what colors they are? (Call on a child. Idea: *Red, yellow, brown and spotted.*)
- Color the birds.
  Then color the rest of the picture.
- Everybody, what color is Sweetie? (Signal.) *Yellow.*
- That eagle is brown and white. The brown parts are a little darker, but they are not brown. You'll have to color them brown.

The Sweetie and the Birdbath story is reread in

several other lessons. Each lesson has a new workbook activity that involves some part of the story. The purpose of the re-readings of each story is to thoroughly acquaint children with details of each story grammar.

EXTENDING STORY GRAMMAR

Extension Stories

For the major story characters, extensions or extrapolations follow the original story. Some new story extensions involve familiar characters and the same basic story grammar as the original story.

The first extension stories appear in lesson 11. The story involves a character named Paul who, in an earlier story, painted things purple. When paint dripped on something near where Paul was painting, he solved the problem by painting it purple. Here's the extension activity from lesson 11.

To tell the story, children follow the basic story grammar. For example, "When Paul is painting the piggy bank, some paint flew over and landed on the pillow. He said, `That looks bad, but I know how to fix it,' and he did. He painted the whole pillow pink . . . ."

The illustrations for extensions are designed so that they have lots of hidden features. In this picture, for instance, many things that aren't labeled are p-starting words. In the picture are palm trees, pyramids, polka dots, a poodle with paws and a parrot on a perch. You may decide to point out some of these objects to the children.

Other Stories

Other story sequences in the program follow the format of having unique story grammars. The characters include Roger (who loves hats but always has problems with them), Roxie (who collects rocks) and Andrea (a shy little mouse who is friends with a dog named Honey, but who hates Sweetie).

Data Collection

In some lessons, children summarize data. They write data in tables that are similar to tables used in math projects. The focus of data collection in the program is on the "truth" of statements that characters make about different data-generating situations.

Here's the first part of the exercise from lesson 42 and the children's workbook page:

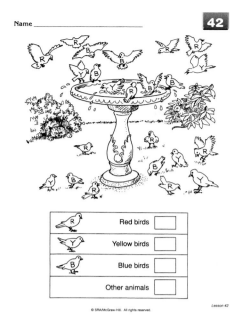

Lesson 42

1. You've heard a story about a woman named Bonnie who bought a birdbath for her yard.

One day, Bonnie was talking to her neighbors. Bonnie said, "I always have red birds and yellow birds and blue birds in my yard. But there are always more red birds than any other color."

One neighbor said, "No, that's not true. I've looked in your yard many times when I was trying to find Sweetie. And I know for a fact that there are always more yellow birds than any other color."

"Not true," another neighbor said. "Every time I've looked in your yard while walking my wonderful dog, Honey, I've always seen more blue birds than birds of any other color."

- If the wise old rat heard this conversation, how do you think he'd go about finding the right answer? (Call on a child. Idea: *Count the birds.*)
- Yes, the smart way is to find out the answer by counting the birds. So **you** can be smart.

2. Look at the picture for part D. The letters on the birds show what color they should be. The letter **R** on a bird shows that the bird should be red.

- Your turn: Take out your **red** crayon and put a **red** mark on all the birds that have the letter **R** on them. Don't miss any birds, but do it fast and don't color the whole bird. Just put a red mark on each bird inside the picture that has an **R** on it. Don't color the bird in the big box. Raise your hand when you're finished.
(Observe children and give feedback.)

3. Now look at the box below the picture. You'll see a picture of a bird with an R on it.
- Touch that bird. ✔
Right after that bird are the words **red birds.** Then there's an empty box. Write the number of **red** birds in that box. Count all the red birds in the picture and write that number in the top box. Raise your hand when you're finished.
(Observe children and give feedback.)
- Everybody, what number did you write for the **red** birds? (Signal.) *Ten.*

4. Now do the same thing for the **yellow** birds. Make a **yellow** mark on every bird in the picture that has the letter Y on it. The **Y** is for **yellow.** After you make your yellow marks, count the yellow birds and write that number in the box for **yellow** birds. Raise your hand when you're finished.
(Observe children and give feedback.)
- Everybody, what number did you write for the **yellow** birds? (Signal.) *Six.*

5. Now do the same thing for the **blue** birds. Make a **blue** mark on every bird in the picture that has the letter **B** on it. The **B** is for **blue.** After you make your **blue** marks, count the **blue** birds and write that number in the box for **blue** birds. Raise your hand when you're finished.
(Observe children and give feedback.)
- Everybody, what number did you write? (Signal.) *Seven.*

6. Get ready to read your numbers one more time.
- Listen: How many **red** birds are in the picture? (Signal.) *Ten.*
- How many **yellow** birds are in the picture? (Signal.) *Six.*

- How many **blue** birds are in the picture? (Signal.) *Seven.*
7. Let's see who was right about the birds in Bonnie's yard. Here's what Bonnie said: "There are always more **red** birds than any other color."
- Think about it. Is that statement true or false? (Signal.) *True.*
- One neighbor said, "There are always more **yellow** birds than any other color." Is that statement true or false? (Signal.) *False.*
- Another neighbor said that there are always more **blue** birds than any other color. Is that statement true or false? (Signal.) *False.*
- So who was right, Bonnie or one of her neighbors? (Signal.) *Bonnie.*
8. Before we leave this picture, there's one more box to fill out below the picture, but I really don't know what goes in there.
- Touch the last box below the picture. ✔ It says, **other animals.** I guess they want you to write the number of other animals that are in the picture. But I really don't see any. Maybe you do. Look at the picture very carefully. See if you can find any other animals in the picture. Count up any animals that are **not** birds and write that number in the last box. If you don't find any other animals, you can write **zero** in the box. Raise your hand when you have a number in the last box. **(Observe children and give feedback.)**
- Everybody, what number did you write for **other animals?** (Signal.) *Two.*
- I guess they were hiding in the picture. I didn't see them.
9. Later, you can color everything in part D.

Children mark each bird with its appropriate color (red for R, yellow for Y and blue for B). Then they count the number of each type of bird and write the number in the "table" at the bottom of the page. In lessons 50 and 87 the children also summarize data to determine the truth of statements that characters make.

SEQUENCING AND RETELLING STORIES

In lesson 7, children are introduced to the first sequencing activity that presents a single picture with numbers. The teacher describes what happens within the scene. Children touch the numbers. Then children retell the sequence by moving to the numbers in order and telling what happens at each number.

1. I'm going to tell you a story about a girl named Rita. You're going to touch the circles I tell you about. Then I'll see who can tell the story to me.
- Listen: Rita is trying to get across the stream without getting wet. So here's what she does first: She backs up.
- Everybody, what does she do first? (Signal.) *Backs up.*
2. One of the circles shows where she goes when she backs up. Touch the circle that shows where she is when she backs up. ✔
- Everybody, what number is in that circle? (Signal.) *One.* That's what Rita does first.
3. After Rita backs up, she runs to the bank of the stream.
- Everybody, what does she do? (Signal.)

Runs to the bank of the stream.
- Touch the circle that shows where she is when she's at the bank of the stream. ✔
- Everybody, what number is in that circle? (Signal.) *Two.*
4. Let's go back to the beginning. First Rita backs up. Touch the circle. ✔
- Then Rita runs to the bank. Touch the circle. ✔
- Now Rita jumps and lands on the big rock in the middle of the stream.
- Everybody, where does she land? (Signal.) *On the big rock.*
- Touch the circle that shows where she lands. ✔
  Everybody, what number is in that circle? (Signal.) *Three.*
5. Then Rita jumps from the big rock and lands on the **other** bank of the stream. She lands on the **other** bank of the stream.
- Everybody, where does she land? (Signal.) *On the other bank of the stream.*
- Touch the circle that shows where she lands. ✔
- Everybody, what number is in that circle? (Signal.) *Four.*
6. I'll say the whole thing. Touch the right circles.
- First, Rita backs up. What number is in the circle? (Signal.) *One.*
- Next, Rita runs to the bank. What number is in the circle? (Signal.) *Two.*
- Next, Rita jumps and lands on the big rock. What number is in the circle? (Signal.) *Three.*
- Next, Rita jumps from the big rock and lands on the other bank of the stream. What number is in the circle? (Signal.) *Four.*
7. Let's see who can tell the story without making any mistakes. Remember, you have to tell what Rita did at each number.
- (Call on a child:) You tell the story. Everybody else, touch the numbers and make sure that (child's name) tells the right thing for each number.

(Praise child for telling what happened at each circle. Repeat with several children.)
8. Everybody, I'm going to ask you some hard questions about Rita.
- Touch the circle that shows Rita on the rock. ✔
- Everybody, what number is in the circle you're touching? (Signal.) *Three.*
- Now touch the circle that shows where Rita went just **after** she was on the rock. ✔
- Everybody, what number is in the circle you're touching? (Signal.) *Four.*
- Now touch the circle that shows where Rita was when she backed up. ✔
- Everybody, what number is in the circle you're touching? (Signal.) *One.*
- Now touch the circle that shows where Rita went just **after** she backed up. ✔
- Everybody, what number is in the circle you're touching? (Signal.) *Two.*
9. Later you can color the picture of Rita.

Teaching Notes

This activity is possibly more difficult than it looks. The reason is that children must mentally alter the picture to figure out what Rita did. The picture shows her standing close to the bank. But the numbers suggest her doing other things and being in other places. Don't be surprised if some children have trouble recounting the story in step 7. If a child has trouble telling the story, prompt by telling the child to touch the next number (or touch number 3) and tell what happened at that number.

If a lot of children have trouble recounting the story or answering the questions in step 8, repeat the activity at another time, possibly before the next lesson. Tell the children, "This is tough. Let's see who can do all the hard things I tell you to do…"

Beginning in lesson 13, children write numbers to show the sequence of events in a story the teacher tells. (In lesson 13, the teacher tells a story about Paul painting a purple parrot.)

During the first reading of the story, children touch the circles that show where the paint dripped first, next and so forth. Then children write the appropriate numbers in the circles. Children retell the story and then color all the things Paul painted purple.

Teaching Notes

Children's interest in the story generally assures that they will attend to the details. However, when presenting the activity, it's a good idea to circulate among the children to make sure they are touching the appropriate places and later writing the numbers appropriately.

There are also sequence exercises in which the children retell a story.

Here's the workbook page for lesson 48. Children refer to the sequence of the four pictures as they retell the central part of the story about *Sweetie and the Birdbath.*

CHARACTER IDENTIFICATION

Some extrapolation activities involve identifying characters by what they say. Here's part of an activity from lesson 70. (Before this part of the exercise, children have identified the pictures and the first letter of each character's name.)

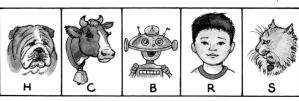

1. _____
2. _____
3. _____
4. _____
5. _____

8. Everybody, touch number 1 and keep touching it. ✔
- Listen and don't say anything. Here's the statement for number 1: "I'd love to go roller-skating just like those children are doing."
- Find the character who would say that. Write the letter for that character on line 1. Raise your hand when you're finished. (Observe children and give feedback.)
9. Everybody, which character would love to go roller-skating just like the children? (Signal.) *Clarabelle.*
- So what letter did you write for number 1? (Signal.) *C.*
- (Write on the board:)

   1. C

- Here's what you should have for number 1. Raise your hand if you got it right. ✔
10. Everybody, touch number 2. ✔
  Listen and don't say anything. Here's the statement for number 2: "Look at those little chicks. Yum, yum."
- Find the character who would say that. Write the letter for that character on line 2. Raise your hand when you're finished. (Observe children and give feedback.)
11. Everybody, which character would say, "Look at those little chicks. Yum, yum"? (Signal.) *Sweetie.*
- So what letter did you write for number 2? (Signal.) *S.*
- (Write to show:)
  1. **C**

  2. **S**

- Here's what you should have for number 2. Raise your hand if you got it right. ✔
12. Everybody, touch number 3. ✔
- Listen and don't say anything. Here's the statement for number 3: "When I sat down, my hat was right over there; but now, I don't know where it is."
- Find the character who would say that. Write the letter for that character on line 3. Raise your hand when you're finished. (Observe children and give feedback.)
13. Everybody, which character would have trouble finding a hat? (Signal.) *Roger.*
- So what letter did you write for number 3? (Signal.) *R.*
- (Write to show:)
  1. **C**

  2. **S**

  3. **R**

- Here's what you should have for number 3. Raise your hand if you got it right. ✔

Starting in lesson 55, children also work cooperatively in groups to develop unique utterances for familiar story characters.

STORY COMPLETION AND PLAYS

Beginning in lesson 77, children make up endings to stories that are based on familiar story grammars. For these activities, you read the first part of a story about Sweetie and the mirror. Sweetie, who had never encountered a mirror that went all the way down to the floor, was in a place where he saw such a mirror, but he didn't know it was a mirror. He challenged the cat in the mirror. Every time he moved, the cat in the mirror moved. Here's the story-completion activity and the play that follows.

> Sweetie said to himself, "That cat is ugly, but it has to be the **fastest** cat I ever saw. When I do something, it seems to do the same thing at the same time I do it."
>
> Then Sweetie said to himself, "It's time to teach this cat a lesson." So he crouched down, leaped at the yellow cat and . . .

2. That's all there is to the story. We're going to have to make up the ending ourselves. Remember, Sweetie gets fooled and then he always says something at the end of these stories.
- Here's where the story stops: Sweetie crouched down, leaped at the yellow cat and . . .
- Now think of what happened to fool Sweetie. Tell what happened when Sweetie jumped. Then tell what Sweetie **thought** happened and what Sweetie said at the end of the story. (Call on several children. Praise ideas such as: *Sweetie bonked himself on the mirror. Then Sweetie said something like, "That yellow cat may be ugly, but he sure can hit hard and fast."*)
3. So here's an ending to the story. See if this is a good one.

> Sweetie crouched down and leaped at the yellow cat. Bonk. Sweetie banged his head against the mirror and went flying. He rolled around on the floor and finally sat up and looked at the cat in the mirror. Sweetie said to himself, "That sure is an ugly cat, but let me tell you, that cat is fast and that cat can really hit hard."

EXERCISE 10

PUTTING ON A PLAY

Sweetie and the Mirror

1. Let's see if we have two children who can act out that story about Sweetie. One child will play Sweetie. The other child will play the cat in the mirror.
- (Call on two children. Tell one:) You're Sweetie.
  (Tell the other:) You're the cat in the mirror. (Have children face each other about 10 feet apart.)
2. Okay, I'll tell each part of the story. Then I'll tell our cats to act out that part.

> Sweetie saw the cat in the mirror. Sweetie arched his back. And the cat in the mirror did the same thing.

- Go cats. ✔

> Next Sweetie made the meanest face he could make. And the cat in the mirror did the same thing.

- Go cats. ✔

> Next Sweetie crouched down and moved toward the yellow cat, closer, closer, closer and the cat in the mirror did the same thing.

- Go cats. ✔

> Now Sweetie held up his **left** paw and showed his claws. And the cat in the mirror held up its **right** paw, the same way.

- Remember, Sweetie, your left paw. Cats go. ✔

> Next Sweetie crouched down and leaped at the yellow cat and went sprawling.

- Cats, be careful and don't really bang into each other. Go. ✔

> Now Sweetie is completely fooled by the mirror and he says something to himself.

- Say it, Sweetie. (Idea: *"That sure is an ugly-looking cat, but let me tell you, that cat is fast and that cat can really hit hard."*)
3. That was pretty good. Maybe next time, we can do it again with a different Sweetie and a different cat in the mirror.

Summary

Here are important points about the story-grammar-activities presented in Grade 1 Language Arts.

1. The grammars prepare children for comprehension activities in many of the stories they will read. Well-written stories present characters that have distinguishing features, that reason and dream, that do things to reach goals. These stories present problems or conflicts and outcomes that are largely implied by the story details. Children who have learned the various grammars presented in Grade 1 Language Arts have a working understanding of a full range of story grammars. This working knowledge helps children focus their attention on details of stories they read, make predictions that are implied by the details of stories and characters, and engage more actively in stories than children who are less sophisticated in story construction.
2. The grammars prepare children for writing activities. Although extensive story writing does not begin until Second Grade, the early work on grammars provides children with the basic knowledge they need to be constructors of interesting stories, not merely critics or categorizers of story details. By the end of First Grade, they will have engaged in many "construction" activities (participating in plays, making up oral stories) that require applying knowledge of the various grammars.
3. Many story-grammars presented in First

Grade are not the type that can be easily summarized in terms of setting, character, problem and so forth. The reason is that each grammar presents characters who have a unique way of thinking and behaving. Consider the Bragging Rats. What is their "problem"? Part of their problem is their "personalities," their ineffective way of settling arguments and their undaunted tendencies to ignore data and to lie. Part of their problem is the particular situation associated with their argument.

Knowledge of the "Bragging Rat format" goes far beyond simple summaries or labels of plot and character. That the children are able to perform on extensive extrapolation activities by the end of the program provides evidence that they have learned much more about story grammar than what is typically taught to children who are much older than they are.

4. Perhaps most important, the children "love" the stories. Part of the reason has to do with the characters. They are not necessarily wonderful, sharing individuals who do everything that is sweet and wholesome. Instead, they get in trouble and make mistakes—two qualities that the children readily identify with.

STORY-RELATED WRITING

Sentence Construction and Writing

Early sentence writing activities show children the relationship between words and specific "ideas." Before children write, they construct word-picture sentences for different illustrations. Here's an example from lesson 53:

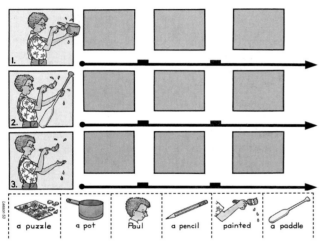

1. Everybody, open your workbook to Lesson 53. Write your name at the top of the page. ✔
2. The pictures show what Paul did. You're going to make up sentences that tell what he did.
3. Look at the cutouts at the bottom of the page. There are words at the bottom of each cutout. I'll read the words.
- Touch the first cutout. ✔
  The words say: **a puzzle.**
- Touch the next cutout. ✔
  The words say: **a pot.**
- Touch the next cutout. ✔
  The word says: **Paul.**
- Touch the next cutout. ✔
  The words say: **a pencil.**
- Touch the next cutout. ✔
  The word says: **painted.**

- Touch the last cutout. ✔
  The words say: **a paddle.**
4. Your turn: Cut out the pictures at the bottom of the page along the dotted lines. Raise your hand when you have all your cutouts ready.
  (Observe children and give feedback.)
5. Everybody, touch picture 1. ✔
- That picture shows something Paul did. What did he do in that picture? (Signal.) *Painted a pot.*
- Here's the sentence that tells Paul did: **Paul painted a pot.**
6. Everybody, say that sentence. (Signal.) *Paul painted a pot.*
  (Repeat step 6 until firm.)
7. (Write on the board:)

- You're going to use your cutout pictures to show that sentence. Here's how you'll do it: You'll put the cutouts for picture 1 in the three boxes next to picture 1.
- (Write **Paul painted** in the first and second boxes on the board:)

Paul	**painted**	

Listen: **Paul painted** a pot.
- (Touch the first box.) So you put the cutout for **Paul** here.
- (Touch the second box.) Then you put the cutout for **painted** here.
- Do that much. Put the cutouts for **Paul** and **painted** in the first two boxes. The words are on the cutouts. Raise your hand when you're finished.
  (Observe children and give feedback.)
8. Everybody, touch picture 1 again. ✔
- Say the whole sentence for that picture. (Signal.) *Paul painted a pot.*

- Fix up the cutouts by putting the right cutout in the last box. Remember, you want your cutouts to say: **Paul painted a pot.** Raise your hand when you're finished.
  (Observe children and give feedback.)
- Everybody, what picture did you put in the last box? (Signal.) *A pot.*
- (Write to show:)

- Here's what the words in your boxes should say. Raise your hand if you got it right. ✔
9. Your turn: Everybody, touch the **arrow** for picture 1. ✔
- Listen: Write the sentence on the arrow for picture 1. Write the words **Paul, painted, a pot.** Those words are written on the bottom of your cutouts. **Paul painted a pot.** Write the whole sentence. Copy the words carefully. Raise your hand when you're finished.
  (Observe children and give feedback.)
- Take your cutouts off the first arrow. ✔
10. Now you're going to make up a sentence for picture 2.
- Everybody, touch picture 2. ✔
  That picture shows something else Paul did. Raise your hand when you can say the whole sentence about what Paul did in picture 2. ✔
11. Everybody, say the sentence. (Signal.) *Paul painted a paddle.*
- (Repeat step 11 until firm.)
12. Put the cutouts in place in the three boxes next to picture 2.
- Make up the sentence: **Paul painted a paddle.** Raise your hand when you're finished.
  (Observe children and give feedback.)
- (Write on the board:)

- Here's what the words should say for picture 2. Raise your hand if you got it right. ✔

- Your turn: Everybody, touch the **arrow** for picture 2. ✔
- Listen: Write the sentence on the arrow for picture 2. Write the words **Paul, painted, a paddle.** Those words are written on the bottom of your cutouts. **Paul painted a paddle.** Write the whole sentence. Copy the words carefully. Raise your hand when you're finished.
  (Observe children and give feedback.)
- Take your cutouts off the second arrow. ✔

The activity requires children to express a single picture as a series of segmented ideas, each expressed by a word unit. Picture 1 shows Paul painting a pot. To express the idea, the children first name Paul, then indicate what he did. The worksheet picture doesn't show what Paul painted in the last picture. After children have completed sentences for the first two pictures and copied the sentences on the arrow below each row of cut-outs, they have an opportunity to make a sentence for the last picture.

Here's the script:

13. Oh, dear. There's another picture of Paul on the page, but the picture doesn't show what Paul painted. Maybe you could make up a sentence about what Paul did by using your cutouts.
- Put your cutouts in the boxes for picture 3 so you make up a sentence that tells about something else Paul did. Don't make up one of the sentences you've already written. Raise your hand when you're finished.
  (Observe children and give feedback.)
- (Call on several children:) Read the sentence you made up about Paul. (Praise appropriate sentences.)
14. Everybody, touch the **arrow** for picture 3. ✔
- Listen: Copy the sentence you made up for picture 3. Raise your hand when you're finished.
  (Observe children and give feedback.)
15. Everybody, turn your cutouts over and put them in a pile. Let's see who can read all three of their sentences. (Call on several children. Praise correct responses.)

In later lessons, a variation of the same procedure is used, except that the children do not cut out the pictures and put them in place. Instead, they go over the words, say the sentences for pictures and write the sentences (copying the words from the appropriate boxes). Here's the workbook page from lesson 74 and the last part of the teacher-directed activity. The children have already written their sentences for the first two illustrations.

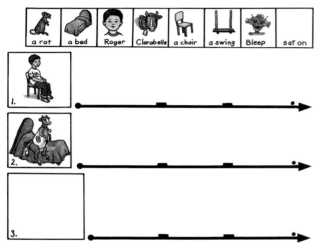

9. There is no picture 3. So here's what you'll do: First you'll make up a sentence that tells what the picture will show. You can write a sentence that uses any of the characters in the boxes. But don't write a sentence we've already done. Write your sentence. Raise your hand when you're finished.

    (Observe children and give feedback.)

10. I'm going to call on several children to read their sentence for picture 3.

- (Call on a child to read sentence 3. Repeat with several children.)
  (Praise original sentences that take the form: *(Name) sat on _____.*)

11. Let's make sure you can read all of your sentences.

- (Call on several children:) Read all three sentences you wrote.
  (Praise children who read appropriate sentences in correct order.)

12. Later, you'll have to draw a picture for sentence 3. Remember, your picture will show what your sentence says.

- (Call on several children:) What will your picture show?
  (Praise those children whose response tells about their sentence.)

13. I'll show you some of the better pictures later.

COOPERATIVE STORY WRITING

Starting in lesson 115, children cooperatively write endings to stories. Children listen to the first part of a story involving Clarabelle: Sixteen frogs were on a log that was floating near the shore of a lake. The frogs were sitting and sunning. Clarabelle saw them and said to herself, "My, that looks like fun. I would love to sit on that log." When she tiptoed into the water, the frogs told her, "Get out of here. Can't you see that this is a frog log, not a cow log?" But when Clarabelle . . . .

After children tell their ending to the story, they dictate an ending to the story, which you write on the board. Then children copy the ending. Lesson 130 provides a model for extending writing assignments beyond the 130 lessons of Grade 1.

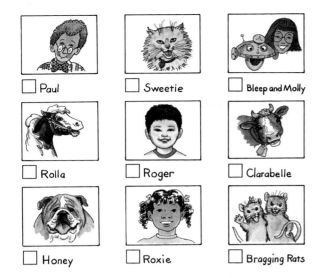

☐ Paul   ☐ Sweetie   ☐ Bleep and Molly

☐ Rolla   ☐ Roger   ☐ Clarabelle

☐ Honey   ☐ Roxie   ☐ Bragging Rats

1. We don't have any more lessons in this program. But we need some more stories for our library, so you're going to write them.
• First we have to figure out which characters we're going to write about.
2. Everybody, open your workbook to lesson 130. Write your name. ✔
   Those are pictures of the characters you've read about. You have to pick your three favorite characters. Those are the characters you'd like to write about most.
• Here's how you do that: You make a check in the box by your three favorite characters. Remember, you can make only three check marks. So look over the characters carefully. Select the three you'd like to write about most and put check marks for those three characters. Remember, only three characters. Do it now.
   (Observe children and give feedback.)
3. Let's see who the all-time favorites are. (Write on the board:)

(Write to show:)

Paul	[ ]
Sweetie	[ ]
Bleep and Molly	[ ]
Rolla	[ ]
Clarabelle	[ ]
Honey	[ ]
Roxie	[ ]
Bragging Rats	[ ]

Paul

• Raise your hand if you made a check for Paul. ✔
  (Count children's raised hands. Write the number after Paul.)
• (Repeat step 3 for the rest of the characters:)
4. (Announce the three winning characters.)
5. (Assign children to four teams.)
   We'll work in teams to make up one good story today. Each team should get together and decide which of the three characters they want to tell about today.
• Talk to your teammates and agree on one of the three winning characters. Raise your hands when you're finished. ✔
• (Ask each team which character they want to tell about.)
6. Now each team is going to work together to make up a good story about the character you chose. Remember, the stories you make up must be the right kind of story for the character. So work out the details. Then each team will tell their story to me. I'll write it. We'll see if each team can come up with a great story. (Observe teams and give feedback. Praise teams that consider different ideas. Praise cute ideas.)

Note: The rest of the lesson may be spread out over several days.

7. (Direct each team to dictate a story. Write it on the board or on a piece of paper to be duplicated.)
   (For later assignments:
   a) teams can make up a story for one of the other characters;
   b) children can individually copy and illustrate one or more of the stories;
   c) teams can make up a story based on a made-up character not introduced in the program.)

MAIN IDEA SENTENCE WRITING

Starting with lesson 80, children compose and write "main-idea" sentences. The sentences they write are in pairs. Some of the sentences rhyme; others don't. All of the sentence pairs are generated from pictures that you discuss with the children.

Here's the teacher and student material for the first sentence pair from lesson 80:

cone   the   fox

The _____

Lesson 80 Side 1

1. Everybody, open your workbook to lesson 80. Write your name at the top of the page. ✔
- You're going to write sentences that rhyme.
- Touch the picture of the fox and the ram. ✔
- The fox had a bone. The ram had something that rhymes with **bone.** What did the ram have? (Signal.) *A cone.* Yes, **the ram had a cone.**
2. Say the sentence for the ram. Get ready. (Signal.) *The ram had a cone.*
- Say the sentence for the fox. Get ready. (Signal.) *The fox had a bone.*
3. (Repeat step 2 until firm.)
4. The word box above the picture shows how to spell the words **cone, the** and **fox.** You can figure out how to spell the other words.

5. Write the sentence for the fox. Remember to start with a capital and end with a period. The first word is already written for you with a capital **T.** Pencils down when you're finished.
(Observe children and give feedback.)
- Now go to the next line and write the sentence for the ram. Pencils down when you're finished.
(Observe children and give feedback.)
6. (Call on individual children to read both their sentences.)

Teaching Notes

Make sure that children's responses are firm on step 2 before moving on. Point out to the children that they will be able to figure out how to spell the other words. If they have trouble spelling a word that is not in the word box, show them how to do it. For example, if they don't know how to spell the word **bone,** tell them, The word **bone** rhymes with **cone.** Look at **cone** and tell me how you spell it Now tell me how to spell **bone.**

Here's an example from lesson 120:

Clarabelle   little   chair   broke

ABCDEFGHIJKLMNO

1.

CDEFGHIJKLMNOPQ

2.

1. You're going to write a sentence about each picture. The word box shows some of the words you may want to use in your sentences. Follow along as I read the words: **Clarabelle, little, chair, broke.**

2. Touch picture 1. ✔
   That shows what Clarabelle did. What did she do? (Call on a child. Ideas: *Sat on a little chair; Clarabelle sat down on a child's chair.*)
- Start with the name **Clarabelle** and say a sentence for picture 1. (Call on a child. Idea: *Clarabelle sat on a little chair.*)
- Everybody, write your sentence for picture 1. Pencils down when you're finished. (Observe children and give feedback.)
- (Call on individual children to read their sentence for picture 1.)
3. Touch picture 2. ✔
   That picture shows what happened to the chair. Start with the words **the chair** and tell what it did. (Call on a child. Ideas: *The chair fell apart. The chair broke.*)
- Write your sentence for picture 2. Start with the words **the chair.** Pencils down when you're finished.
   (Observe children and give feedback.)
- (Call on individual children to read their sentence for picture 2.)
4. (Collect papers. Marks errors in spelling, punctuation, and clarity.)

For the first picture, children write a sentence that starts with the name **Clarabelle** and tells what she did in the picture. For the second picture, children write a sentence that tells what happened to the chair when Clarabelle sat in it.

Appendix A— Placement Test

How to Administer the Test

1. Plan to administer the entry test individually to each child who has not been taught the kindergarten language program. Allow three to five minutes for each child you will test.
2. Make a copy of the score sheet on page 99 for each child.
3. Familiarize yourself with the instructions and the score sheet before testing.
4. Sit at the same side of a low table with the child, preferably in a quiet corner of the room.
5. Score the child's response on the score sheet as you present each test item. Circle 0 to indicate a correct response to a test item and 1 to indicate an incorrect response. Each error counts as 1 and the child's score is the total number of errors he or she makes.
6. Stop testing as soon as a child makes six errors and if possible, give the test for the Kindergarten Language Program. If a child makes five or fewer errors, he or she can begin instruction in Grade 1 Language Arts.

Part 1

(Place a sheet of paper on the table. Hand the child a penny. If the child answers "there" in any of the following tasks, say:) Tell me **where** it is.

1. Put the penny on the piece of paper. (Wait.) Tell me. **Where** is the penny? (The child is to put the penny on the paper and say, *On the paper.*)
2. Now hold the penny over the piece of paper. (Wait.) Tell me. **Where** is the penny now? (The child is to hold the penny so that it is over the piece of paper, but not touching, and say, *Over the paper.*)
3. Now put the penny next to the piece of paper. (Wait.) Tell me. **Where** is the penny now? (The child is to put the penny next to the paper and say, *Next to the paper.*)
4. Put the penny under the piece of paper. (Wait.) Tell me. **Where** is the penny now? (The child is to put the penny under the paper and say, *Under the paper.*)

End of Part 1

Part 2

I'll say sentences. Say them just the way I say them.

5. Listen. (Pause.) If it rains, the cows will get wet. Say that. (Repeat the statement once if the child fails on the first attempt. If the child repeats the statement correctly either the first or second trial, score the item correct.)
6. Listen. (Pause.) They were having a good time on their vacation. Say that. (Repeat the statement once if the child fails on the first attempt. If the child repeats the statement correctly on the first or second trial, score the item correct.)

End of Part 2

Part 3

Look at the picture.
7. Two of these elephants are **wearing** the same thing. Point to the two elephants that are **wearing** the same thing.
(The child is to point to elephant 1 and elephant 3.)
8. What are they wearing that is the same? (The child is to respond *hats* or *a hat*.)
9. Two of these elephants are **holding** the same thing. Point to the two elephants that are **holding** the same thing.
(The child is to point to elephant 1 and elephant 2.)
10. What are they holding that is the same? (The child is to respond *flowers* or a *flower*.)
End of Part 3

Part 4

Tell me if I hold up some of my fingers, all of my fingers, or none of my fingers. (If the child identifies the *number* of fingers in any of the following tasks, ask:) Am I holding up some of my fingers, all of my fingers, or none of my fingers?
11. (Hold up all ten fingers.) What am I holding up? (The child is to respond *all of your fingers* or *all*.)
12. (Hold up seven fingers.) What am I holding up? (The child is to respond *some of your fingers* or *some*.)
13. (Hold up three fingers.) What am I holding up? (The child is to respond *some of your fingers* or *some*.)
14. (Hold up a closed fist.) What am I holding up? (The child is to respond *none of your fingers* or *none*.)
End of Part 4

Part 5

I'm going to tell you a story about a tiger. I'm going to tell the story one time. So listen carefully. Here is the story. The tiger lived in the jungle. The tiger hunted at night. The tiger did not hunt during the day. It slept all day long.
(Accept all reasonable responses to the following items.)
15. Who hunted? *The tiger.*
16. Where did the tiger live? *In the jungle.*
17. When did the tiger hunt? *At night.*
18. When did the tiger sleep? *In the day.*
19. What did the tiger do during the day? *Slept* or *Sleeping.*
20. What did the tiger do during the night? *Hunted* or *Hunt.*
End of Part 5

PLACEMENT TEST SCORE SHEET Grade 1 Language Arts

This test is to be given only to those children who have not been taught *Grade K Language.* Stop testing as soon as a child makes six errors. Give that child the *Grade K Language* Placement Test.

Student's name _____

Date _____

Items	Correct Responses	Incorrect Responses
PART 1		
1	0	1
2	0	1
3	0	1
4	0	1
PART 2		
5	0	1
6	0	1
PART 3		
7	0	1
8	0	1
9	0	1
10	0	1
PART 4		
11	0	1
12	0	1
13	0	1
14	0	1
PART 5		
15	0	1
16	0	1
17	0	1
18	0	1
19	0	1
20	0	1

Total Score _____

Appendix B—
Reproducible Calendar

This reproducible calendar is for language arts lessons with calendar activities.
Note: Fill in your monthly calendar in two stages. First fill in the current month.

(sample Month)   <u>__September</u>

Sunday	Monday	Tuesday	Wednesday	Thursday	Friday	Saturday
					1	2
3	4	5	6	7	8	9
10	11	12	13	14	15	16
17	18	19	20	21	22	23
24	25	26	27	28	29	30

From Lesson 33 until the End of the program, children are asked to say the date that is one week from today. Fill in the first part of the upcoming month when this information is called for in the lesson.

<u>__September</u>

Sunday	Monday	Tuesday	Wednesday	Thursday	Friday	Saturday
					1	2
3	4	5	6	7	8	9
10	11	12	13	14	15	16
17	18	19	20	21	22	23
24	25	26	27	28	29	30

October

1	2	3	4	5	6	7

Sunday	Monday	Tuesday	Wednesday	Thursday	Friday	Saturday	

	Objectives	Lessons
Actions	Generate a complete sentence to describe an action and follow directions involving if-then.	10, 11
	Label actions, and follow directions involving "all," "some" and "none," generate complete sentences to describe an action and answer questions involving "or."	12, 13
	Generate statements to describe actions using present, past and future tense.	15, 17-19, 21, 27-29, 37, 42, 50, 51, 53, 54, 63
	Generate statements to describe actions using prepositional phrases and make statements and answer questions involving "or."	16
	Label actions, follow directions involving "all," "some" and "none," and generate complete sentences to describe an action using past, present and future tense.	20, 22
	Follow directions for and discriminate between same and different actions.	23, 30
	Given a common noun, name the class.	31-33
	Name classes and subclasses.	32-35, 38-40, 64
	Describe actions involving same/different, and from/to.	52
	Name three classes, containing a common noun and answer questions about members of those classes.	32, 38, 52, 53, 55, 65, 75, 104, 105
	Generate statements to describe actions involving "before" and "after."	69
Classification	Identify objects in a large class, in the classes of plants and animals, in the class of vehicles; in subclasses and classes; in the class of food; in the class of tools.	1; 2–4, 6; 2; 3
	Identify classes; and name objects in those classes.	4–6; 8–13
	Ask questions involving "class" and "parts" to figure out a "mystery" object.	18
	Given classes, order classes by "biggest," "next biggest," and "smallest," answer questions about the classes and given members of a class, identify the class.	21-26
	Given two classes, identify which class is biggest, describe why and name members of the biggest class.	28-32, 34-36
	Answer classification questions involving "only" and name members of the given class.	38
	Answer classification questions involving true, false and only.	38-40
	Given a common noun, name three classes containing the noun (smallest, next).	41-46
	Name four classes containing a common noun and answer questions about members of those classes.	47, 60, 73, 89, 107
	Given a common noun, name four classes containing the noun.	47-50
	Use clues to eliminate members of a familiar class.	82, 85, 88
	Write class names next to members of the class.	89, 93, 95, 97, 102, 103, 107, 110, 112, 117, 125, 129
	Name members of a class and subclass and identify the bigger class.	71, 79, 81, 88, 101, 103

Word Skills

	Objectives	Lessons
Opposites	Name common opposites and answer questions by generating sentences using opposites.	1-7, 9-13, 17-28, 30, 39
	Name common opposites, answer questions by generating sentences using opposites and generate a sentence that means the opposite of a given sentence.	29
	Name common opposites.	40, 63-65, 68, 72, 98, 100, 130
	Generate a statement with the opposite of a given word.	37, 58
Definitions	Identify common nouns given simple definitions.	7

	Given a common noun, construct a definition by naming the class and saying something true of only that noun.	41-43
	Generate a list of objects that fit stated criteria.	47, 48, 58, 59
	Identify an object based on its characteristics.	65, 67, 69, 71-73, 75-82, 85-99, 106, 109, 110, 112, 130
Synonyms	Recite the definition of "synonym."	77
	Replace a word in a sentence with a synonym.	77-79, 81, 83-91, 94, 97, 99-103, 105, 110-116, 118, 119, 123
	Name common synonyms.	80, 91, 92, 96, 116, 117
	Replace a word in a sentence with a synonym and generate sentences using synonyms for given words.	83
	Discriminate between synonyms and opposites.	86, 95, 97, 98, 106, 107, 122, 129
	Name common synonyms and opposites.	91, 96
	Replace a word in a sentence with an opposite.	101, 111, 113
	Follow directions involving synonyms.	111
	Read a word and write the opposite of that word.	112, 113, 116, 121, 125, 126, 128
Contraction	Replace words in a sentence with appropriate contractions.	120-124
	Generate sentences with contractions.	126-130

Sentence Skills

How-Who-What Where-When- Why	Follow directions and identify statements that tell "where."	2-4, 6, 7
	Follow directions, make statements and answer questions involving "and" and "or."	5
	Identify statements that tell "when" and where and discriminate between the statements that tell "when" and those that tell "where."	6-8, 14
	Identify statements that tell "when" and "where" and generate statements that tell "when" and "where"; and statements that tell "when something is not"; and statements that tell when something did not occur; and statements that tell "not when something occurred".	9; 11, 12; 17; 18, 20, 22
	Given a complex sentence, answer questions involving "who," "why," "when" and "what"; "who," "when," and "where".	31; 20, 21, 24, 25, 27, 28
	Given a common noun, name the class.	31-33
	Given a complex sentence, answer questions involving "who," "when" and "why"; "who," "what" and "why"; "where," "what" and "why"; "where," "who" and "why"; "who," "how" and "why"; "who," "what," "how," and "why".	32; 33; 34; 33, 35; 36; 40;
	Given a short statement, generate an expanded sentence that tells "why," "when" or "where."	36, 37
	Given a complex sentence, answer questions involving "who," "how," why and "where."	36, 37
	Given two sentences, identify which gives more information and if it tells "where," "why," or "when."	37
	Given a complex sentence, answer questions involving "why" and discriminate between statements that tell "where" and "why."	40
	Generate statements utilizing past, present and future tenses of the verb "to be."	43, 46, 48, 59
	Listen to a short story and answer questions involving "who," "when," "why," "where" and "what".	45-48, 74, 76, 85, 86, 89, 91, 92, 94, 95, 99, 104, 112, 120, 127
	Given a complex sentence, answer questions involving who, what, where, when and why.	61, 62
Questioning Skills	Ask questions involving "material," "use" and "parts" to figure out a "mystery" object.	20-23, 25-36

Given a common noun, generate questions and statements involving class, use, and location. (Ex. 6)	38
Apply narrowing criteria to guess a mystery object.	48, 49, 50, 52, 57, 58, 64, 112, 126
Identify an word based on its characteristics.	100, 101, 103, 105, 107, 108, 115-120, 123-129
Generate questions to find a word's definition.	83, 85, 86, 87, 90, 92, 94, 96, 99, 107, 109, 113, 118, 121, 127

Verb Tense

Identify past and future tense; past and present tense; past, present and future tense.	98; 101, 102; 109, 110, 112, 114, 122–124
Identify and generate sentences involving past, present and future tense.	50, 119
Generate a sentence with past tense; past and future tense; past, present and future tense.	121; 123; 124, 128, 130

Statements

Name things that a statement does NOT tell.	59, 63, 65, 67, 70, 95, 96, 98, 105, 118, 122, 125, 128, 129
Given two statements, tell which one tells more about what happened and why it tells more.	72

Reasoning Skills

Same-Different

Follow directions involving if-then and discriminate between same and different actions.	8, 9, 14
Name ways that two common objects are the same and/or different.	8-17
Discriminate between same and different actions.	74
Identify how common objects are the same and different.	77, 79

True-False

Identify true and false statements involving common objects.	14-17
Given two objects, identify whether a statement is true of "only one" or "both" objects and generate a statement that is true of both objects.	26, 27
Given a common object, answer true/false questions.	41, 45
Given a common object, answer true/false questions and generate true/false statements.	42-44
Discriminate between true and false statements and generate true and false statements.	49, 53, 56, 57, 61, 74, 75, 76, 77, 78

Can Do

Given a common noun, answer questions involving "can do."	41, 42, 44-48, 52-56, 72, 74, 86
Generate statements involving "can do" and "cannot do."	42, 49, 58, 62, 68, 69, 73, 78, 81, 83
Given a common noun, name things that "can" and "cannot" be done with the noun.	45, 47, 48, 50
Given a common object, generate activities that "can" and "cannot do" with the object.	57, 58

Only

Given two objects, identify whether a statement is true of "only one" or "both" objects.	18, 19, 21-23, 25-27, 29
Answer classification questions involving "only" and name members of the given class.	38
Given a common noun, construct a definition by naming the class and saying something true of only that noun.	41-43

Description

Identify a place based on its characteristics.	114

Analogies

Complete an analogy involving parts of a whole; location; class.	49; 50; 52, 57, 61, 62, 68
Complete verbal analogies.	65-68
Construct a verbal analogy and repeat the definition of analogy.	69-74, 75, 77-81, 83, 89-91, 93-101, 103, 106, 107, 111, 113, 121, 129
Complete an analogy involving use.	70, 76
Identify the relationship between the components of an analogy.	82-84, 86-88, 102-106, 108-110

If-then	Follow directions involving if-then and discriminate between same and different actions.	44, 45, 47, 48, 59, 126, 130
	Apply an if-then rule based on the occurrence of events.	94, 95, 99, 100, 109, 114
	Construct an if-then rule involving missing parts of a whole.	118, 119

Direction Skills

From-To	Given actions, answer questions involving to and from.	37
	Given a picture, identify an object being moved away "from" and the object being moved "to."	39, 40, 47
	Given an action, answer questions involving movement "from" and "to" and generate statements about the movement.	41, 42, 44, 48
	Follow directions involving "from"/"to."	49
Map Reading	Identify cardinal directions. (North, South, East, West); Identify cardinal directions on a map.	46–51, 82, 83, 85,104; 52, 53, 62, 65, 71
	Label cardinal directions on a map.	84, 90, 93, 98, 101, 102, 104, 108, 110, 117, 122, 126, 128

Information

Days, Months, Seasons	Name the days of the week and the seasons.	2
	Identify days and dates on a calendar.	2-4
	Name the days of the week and the seasons and identify how many months are in a year; and name the first four months of the year; and name the first eight months of the year.	3; 4; 5, 6
	Given a calendar, identify the day and date for "yesterday" and "today"; and name the days of the week. (Ex. 7)	5–13, 15–17, 19–29; 6
	Given a calendar, identify the day and date for "yesterday" and "today" Name the days of the week, the seasons and the twelve months of the year.	7
	Answer questions about previously taught calendar facts and the number of days in a year.	15
	Given a calendar, identify the day and date for "yesterday" and "today."	28
	Given a calendar, identify the day and date for "today" and "tomorrow" and one week from today.	30-56, 63-88, 92, 93, 114
	Identify the number of days in a month and answer questions involving previously learned calendar facts.	83
	Answer questions about previously taught calendar facts.	8-16, 18-20, 23, 26-29, 36-38, 56, 58, 59-62, 75, 84, 89-91, 99, 106, 111, 117, 124
Materials	Identify parts of a common object and the materials it is made of.	16-22, 24, 30
	Identify common materials.	16, 17
	Given a common noun, identify the color and material of the object.	35
	Given a material, name common nouns made of that material.	36
	Name objects that could be made of a given material using true and false statements.	49-51, 53-57, 89, 102, 108, 114

Applications

Absurdities	Answer questions involving absurdity of function.	9
	Generate an absurd sequence for a common activity.	13
	Identify and generate absurdities of location.	17, 23, 47
	Identify and generate absurdities of use.	21, 79, 81, 85, 77, 79
	Identify absurdities involving materials.	76, 77, 79, 80
	Identify absurdities involving condition.	80, 85, 97

Identify absurdities of ability and use.	89
Identify absurdities.	101, 108, 110, 111, 115, 120, 125, 127, 128, 129

Temporal Sequencing	Listen to and retell a sequence of events then correct sequencing errors when the sequence is given out of order.	14-19
	Given a sequence, answer questions about the sequence.	29
	Given a sequence of actions, repeat the sequence, recall and carry out the sequence of actions and answer questions about the sequence.	34, 35
	Given sequenced pictures, retell a familiar story.	36
	Retell a familiar story.	48

Story Grammar and Literature Strand
Story Grammar

Stories	Listen to a new story.	1-3, 12, 21, 28, 33, 38, 43, 45, 49, 54, 58, 65, 66
	Listen to a familiar story.	4-6, 22, 25, 30, 52, 56, 60
	Answer questions about the events in a familiar story.	7, 41, 47, 82
	Answer questions about a familiar story and relate the story to a picture that has numbers showing where the various events occurred.	24, 59
Extending Story Grammar	Answer questions and make predictions about a new story.	44
Character Identification	Identify a familiar story character from unique utterances.	17
	Cooperatively develop utterances for familiar story characters.	96
	Match unique utterances to the familiar story character who would speak them.	57, 70, 72
	Discriminate between good and bad clues for identifying a story character.	118
	Use clues to identify objects referred to in familiar stories, and identify the character described in each clue.	123

Story Completion and Plays

Storytelling Details	Answer questions about a new story.	1-3, 12, 21, 28, 33, 38, 43, 45, 49, 54, 58, 65, 66
	Make a picture consistent with the details of the story.	1-6, 12, 15, 21, 22, 25, 28, 33, 38, 43-45, 49, 52, 54, 62, 69, 77, 79
Sequencing Events	Answer questions about sequence in a familiar story and make a picture consistent with the details of the story.	6, 31, 34
	Relate a sequence of actions of a story character to a picture with numbers (1,2,3,4) showing where each action occurred.	7-9
	Write numbers to show the sequence of events, tell a story based on familiar story grammar and color a picture to make it consistent with the story.	13, 14, 23, 27
	Generate a story given a picture and numbers identifying story events' sequence.	20
	Write numbers to show the sequence of events and tell the story.	23
	Listen to a familiar story and answer questions regarding story sequence.	30
	Given a picture from a familiar story, answer literal, inferential and sequence questions and make the picture consistent with the story.	31, 41
	Make a picture consistent with the details of a story using "beginning" and "end."	33
	Write numbers and draw paths to show a sequence of events and tell a story that involves an interaction of events.	46

	Construct word-picture sentences for story illustrations.	51, 53, 55
Data Collection	Collect data on groups and tell whether statements about groups are true or false.	42, 50, 87
Extrapolation	Relate a familiar story grammar to a picture that indicates the sequence of events for a new story.	11, 16-19, 26, 29, 32, 35, 39, 67, 71, 85
	Relate a familiar story grammar to a picture that indicates the sequence of events for a new story.	67
Putting on a Play	Put on a play to show a new story.	39, 67
	Put on a play to show a familiar story.	40, 60, 69, 77, 79
Skills (Days, Months, Bleep Talk)	Complete a picture by copying the words, to show a familiar character saying the days of the week.	58-60
	Complete a picture by copying the words to show a familiar character saying the months of the year.	65, 66, 68
	Complete a picture by copying the words to show a familiar character saying the months of the year.	68
Story Completion	Make up an ending to a story based on familiar story grammar.	62, 77
	Cooperatively generate an ending to a story.	63, 115, 127
	Listen to part of a familiar story and recall the story ending.	79

Workbook Tracks

Coloring	Follow coloring rules involving shapes; class; specific objects; class and parts of a whole; "some" and "all"; moving "from" and "to"; material; classes and subclasses; "all" and "some"; cardinal directions; smaller and larger classes; classification and using "some" and "all"; "some" and class.	1; 1–3, 5, 8–14, 16, 18, 23, 25, 27, 32, 45, 49; 2; 7; 29; 32, 34–36, 43, 44; 38, 39, 47, 48, 50, 54, 65, 71, 72, 74, 86, 95, 106; 40, 41, 43, 48, 52, 57, 61, 63, 68, 70, 72, 74–76, 80, 83, 84, 86, 90, 108, 111, 116, 119, 122, 124; 29, 45; 54, 56, 58; 104; 38; 56, 58
Part-Whole	Follow coloring rules involving parts of a whole.	4
Writings	Replace a word in a sentence with an opposite.	46

Writing Strand
Story–Related Writing

	Construct word-picture sentences for story illustrations.	51, 53, 55
Sentence Construction and Writing	Write three sentences about story characters. (Ex. 6)	61, 64, 73-76, 78
	Write three sentences.	87
	Write sentences given picture clues.	102
Cooperative Story Writing	Cooperatively write a story about three familiar characters.	130

Main Idea Sentence Writing

Main Idea	Write rhyming sentences given picture cues.	80, 81, 83, 84, 86, 88-93, 96,111,114, 116, 119
	Write sentences given picture cues.	94, 98, 99-101, 103-110, 112, 113, 117, 118, 121, 122, 124, 125, 126, 128, 129

Sequence Sentence Writing

Sequence	Write sentences identifying sequence given picture cues.	120